# POND & RIVER LIFE

A practical guide to animal life in fresh water
described and illustrated in colour

Pamela Forey & Peter Forey

BROCKHAMPTON PRESS

## CAUTION

**Ponds and lakes, streams and rivers, even marshes, are often beautiful and fascinating; but they can also be dangerous and should always be treated with respect. Be aware that rivers can have slippery rocks or strong currents which can sweep you off your feet. The water in gravel pits is cold and deep. Never lean too far out when pond-dipping, even in small ponds. Never try to walk on the mud of muddy river shores, fens and marshes; the mud can be soft and deep and you could be trapped in it. Always keep an eye on young children when they are near water.**

**If you turn over a stone in a stream, make sure you put it carefully back the same way up. Otherwise the animals that were living on its underside may die.**

This edition published in 2000 by
Brockhampton Press,
20 Bloomsbury Street,
London WC1B 3QA,

This edition produced under licence by
Malcolm Saunders Publishing Ltd, London

A CIP Catalogue record for this book is available from the British Library

Title: Pocket Reference Guides, POND & RIVER LIFE
ISBN: 1 86019 782 5

Printed in China by Colorcraft

# Contents

# Introduction

Pond-dipping (dipping nets into ponds and seeing what comes out), or turning over stones in streams to see what is underneath, are two activities that keep children happy for hours. They can also satisfy the curiosity of many adults. This book is designed to provide an introduction to many of the animals you might find in these ways. It also covers some of the larger animals that live in all kinds of fresh water, from mountain streams to big rivers, deep lakes and reservoirs, canals, marshes and ditches, garden ponds and even water butts or puddles.

We cannot hope to include all the species present in the fresh waters of Europe and the British Isles in a book this size, so we have focused on fishes and the other more obvious creatures; but we have also tried to provide a representative sample of all the kinds of animal that live in fresh water, and to give you some idea of how and where they live. Waterfowl and mammals are described in the companion books in this series (*Birds* and *Mammals*) and therefore we have omitted them to make space for creatures not represented in the other books.

# How to use this book

Several groups of animals are included in the book and it has been divided into ten sections to reflect this diversity. The sections are **Reptiles**; **Amphibians**; **Fishes**; **Crustaceans**; **Spiders**; **Insects**; **Molluscs**; **Worms**; **Sponges**; and **Microscopic Animals**. Each section is indicated by a different colour band at the top of the page (see the contents list on the previous page). To identify your animal, first read through the information in the *Guide to identification* and then turn to the relevant page.

# Guide to identification

First decide to which section your organism belongs by reading the following descriptions.

 **REPTILES** (pages 16-17) include snakes, lizards and turtles. Few live in water and only two are included in this book - a **snake** and a **terrapin** (a kind of turtle). They all have dry, hard, scale-covered skin. Snakes have long, cylindrical bodies and no legs; turtles have distinctive 'shells' formed of a domed carapace above the back and a flat section beneath the belly. The shell is made of many interlocking plates.

**AMPHIBIANS** (pages 18-26) include frogs, toads, newts and salamanders. Most have soft, often moist, skin with no scales, although some toads have rough, warty skin. Almost all of them lay their eggs in water and their young are tadpoles.

**Frogs and toads** spend a lot of time on land but may hibernate in water or return to water in hot weather. They have a distinctive shape with short bodies and no tails. They have long hind limbs and many hop or jump. **Newts and salamanders** have long bodies, long tails and relatively short legs. They are wet-skinned and may live on land or in water.

**Tadpoles**, often very common in ponds and ditches, are the young amphibians. They have very soft bodies and begin life with just a head and a tail. As they grow, they develop hind legs and then front legs, then finally change shape to look like tiny adults.

**FISHES** (pages 27-62) are probably the most familiar of aquatic animals and almost need no description. Most of them have the classic, streamlined fish shape, but even the few that do not (like eels or flatfishes, for example) still have the other fishy features - fins on back and belly, paired pectoral and pelvic fins, and a vertical tail fin. They breathe by means of gills; the body is covered by fragile, loose scales.

**Lampreys** (page 63) are eel-like animals that look like fishes (especially like eels) but are really not fishes at all. They lack jaws, have no paired pectoral or pelvic fins and have no scales. They are included in the fish section here for convenience.

**CRUSTACEANS** (pages 64-67) have bodies formed of many segments. They are covered in a hard but (relatively) flexible skeleton, much of the flexibility coming from the joints between each segment. Some crustaceans have bodies formed of many similar segments; in others, the segments are different in the three body sections of head, thorax and abdomen. All crustaceans have jointed legs (these vary in number, but they have at least four pairs and often many pairs of legs), and there are two pairs of antennae on the head.

Marine crustaceans can get quite large, like the crabs and lobsters, but freshwater forms are mostly smaller. They include **water slaters**, **shrimps** and **crayfish**. Many others are microscopic and a few of these are described on page 120.

**SPIDERS** (pages 68-69) also have segmented bodies, but the segments are not obvious; what is more obvious is the division of the body into head and abdomen. They have four pairs of jointed legs, distinctive poison fangs, and spinners on the abdomen to make silk for their webs. Most spiders are terrestrial, but a very few live in or around fresh water.

Mites are related to spiders and also have four pairs of legs, but differ in having a round, not two-part body. **Water mites** are described on page 121.

 **INSECTS** (pages 70-105) are a very large group that includes butterflies and moths, flies, beetles, bees and wasps, bugs, mayflies and dragonflies, as well as many other types. They can be identified by the three sections that make up the body (head, thorax and abdomen). The head bears a single pair of antennae. There are three pairs of jointed legs on the thorax. Many adult insects, for example dragonflies, have two pairs of wings; in beetles the front pair is modified to form the hardened wing cases. Flies have only one functional pair of wings.

Insects have a hard skeleton around the outside of the body like crustaceans and spiders; they grow by losing this skeleton periodically (a process called moulting), and expanding their size rapidly as much as they can before the new skeleton hardens. The new skeleton is formed inside the old one before the insect moults, but stays soft until it comes into contact with the air. Crustaceans and spiders also grow in this way.

Many insects (including most aquatic ones) have a life cycle in which their young lead a very different life style from that of their parents. Often these young look very different from the adults too. They are known as nymphs or larvae. For aquatic insects, this often means that the adults are terrestrial but lay their eggs in water, and their young nymphs or larvae develop in the water, growing and moulting until they reach full size.

When the insects have nymphs as their young, (**mayflies**, **dragonflies and damselflies**, **stoneflies** and **bugs**), the full-grown nymphs moult one last time - and the winged adults emerge from the cast-off skin of the nymph. In these groups the wings can be seen developing gradually as wing-buds on the thorax of the nymph, enlarging slightly at each moult.

Insects that have larvae do it differently. The larvae (or caterpillars as they are called when belonging to moths or butterflies) grow to their full size, moulting often, but never develop wing-buds. When full-grown, they form a pupa or chrysalis, a sort of resting stage, inside which enormous structural changes take place and the adult insect is formed. When the changes are complete, the adult insect emerges. Aquatic insects which have this kind of life style include mosquitoes and other **true flies**, **caddis flies**, **alder flies**, **china-mark moths** and **beetles**.

Insects are a hugely successful group, colonising almost every terrestrial and freshwater habitat on Earth. Their success in water has largely come from this life cycle, where the young can be aquatic while the adults are terrestrial. A few insects, like the aquatic bugs and beetles, have taken to the water totally; but even here the adults are often winged and can fly from pond to pond.

**MOLLUSCS** (pages 106-112) are a large group of animals which include (among others) snails, slugs, cockles and mussels. There are several freshwater species

**Gastropod** molluscs include the familiar snails and slugs. Snails have a soft, unsegmented body covered by a calcareous shell, coiled into a cone in the most familiar forms, like garden snails. However, the shells of water snails are more variable; some, like limpets, have simple conical shells while others, like ramshorns, have the shell coiled in one plane. When the animals emerge from their shells, they have the same gliding foot, and head with tentacles as their land cousins.

**Bivalve** molluscs are very different to gastropods at first glance; internally, however, they share many biological features with them. Most bivalves can be very quickly recognised from their shell, which is divided into two more or less equal valves. They include mussels and cockles.

**WORMS** (pages 113-117). Several different types of worms are included in this book. Many are long and cylindrical(worm-like) in shape, others are flattened and more ribbon-like. Some have bodies divided into segments, while others are unsegmented.

**Segmented worms** have long, worm-like bodies divided into many similar, more or less bristly segments. Some of them, like the *Tubifex* worms, resemble earthworms, with simple, cylindrical bodies. But often the most evident of these worms in fresh water are the more flattened leeches. They can be recognised by their distinctive movement and suckers at both ends of the body.

**Hairworms and Roundworms** both have long, hair-like, unsegmented bodies.

**Planarian worms** do not have cylindrical bodies, but instead come from a group known as flatworms, for obvious reasons. Their bodies are soft and flattened, often arrow-shaped, and they move with a distinctive gliding motion.

**SPONGES** (page 118) may not look like animals at all, but might be mistaken for plants because they do not move about. Or they might not look like living organisms at all. They form crusts on stones and water plants, some with finger-like projections.

**MICROSCOPIC ANIMALS** (pages 119-121). The final section contains various unrelated animals, including hydra, microscopic crustaceans, mites and rotifers). We have grouped them together because you need a microscope to see them clearly. If the organism you are looking at falls into this category, we suggest you turn directly to this section. (See also the section on worms; some of these are very small).

# What's on a page

Once you have decided to which group your organism belongs, turn to the pages on which representative species of that group are described and illustrated. Compare the information on the relevant pages to make a positive identification.

On many of the pages, especially in the fish, amphibian and reptile sections, you will find one species on each page (perhaps with an illustration of a related species that is described in box four). In the other sections, many of the pages are devoted to groups of animals rather than to an individual species. For instance we have included a page on damselflies; by making this a group page we can give you some idea of the range of damselflies found in Europe and the British Isles, even in our limited space.

Throughout the insect section, you will find that both adults and nymphs or larvae are described, often on facing pages. Where the group is particularly large with many species, the first two pages are followed by others to illustrate some of the variety of species within the group.

On each page you will find the name of the species or group at the top. The length of the animal is also given. Four text boxes provide information about the species or group illustrated:

The first box provides details of features or combinations of features, which together with the illustration, make identification possible. The second box provides information on biology, behaviour and what they feed on. The third box provides information on habitat and geographical distribution; an indication is also given here if a species is commercially important. The fourth box gives information about the members of a group if this is a group page; or it may tell you how to identify related or similar species. On some pages related species are also illustrated.

## Other common species

Also scattered throughout the book are pages with a slightly different layout on which two or more species are presented. These are perhaps a little less common than those on the other pages, or are less widely distributed. Nonetheless, you may well encounter them and they are certainly of interest.

## Warning symbol

If the animal could nip, bite or sting you, this warning symbol has been included with the illustration.

## Distribution Map

A distribution map supplements the information in the third text box, giving quick reference to the countries in which the species or group occurs.

- ● - the species or group is common or widespread in this area

- ○ - the species or group is less common in this area, or is found in only part of the area

Note that in the *Insect* section, maps are given only on adult insect pages but are also valid for their nymphs or larvae.

## Specimen page

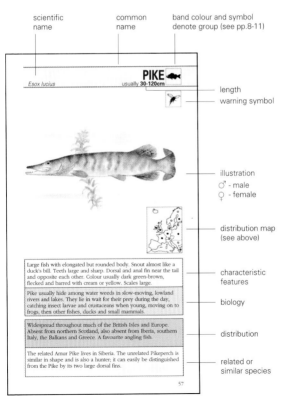

scientific name

common name

band colour and symbol denote group (see pp.8-11)

**PIKE**

*Esox lucius*  usually **30-120cm**

length

warning symbol

illustration
♂ - male
♀ - female

distribution map (see above)

Large fish with elongated but rounded body. Snout almost like a duck's bill. Teeth large and sharp. Dorsal and anal fin near the tail and opposite each other. Colour usually dark green-brown, flecked and barred with cream or yellow. Scales large.

characteristic features

Pike usually hide among water weeds in slow-moving, lowland rivers and lakes. They lie in wait for their prey during the day, catching insect larvae and crustaceans when young, moving on to frogs, then other fishes, ducks and small mammals.

biology

Widespread throughout much of the British Isles and Europe. Absent from northern Scotland, also absent from Iberia, southern Italy, the Balkans and Greece. A favourite angling fish.

distribution

The related Amur Pike lives in Siberia. The unrelated Pikeperch is similar in shape and is also a hunter; it can easily be distinguished from the Pike by its two large dorsal fins.

related or similar species

57

13

# Illustrated glossary

**anal glands** (in a snake) - a pair of glands that open into the anus of a snake. Water Snakes and Grass Snakes empty out the contents of these glands, mixed with excrement, if they are caught.

**columella** (in a snail) - the rod that forms the central axis of the shell.

**invertebrate** - a collective term for all animals which lack a backbone (includes insects, crustaceans, spiders, molluscs and worms, among others).

**keeled** - having a sharp, median ridge.

**parasite** - an organism that lives in or on another living organism (its host) and feeds on the host, usually without killing it.

**parotoid gland** (of a toad) - a glandular swelling on the side of the head behind the eye that secretes a poisonous fluid.

**plankton** - tiny animals and plants that drift near the surface of still or very slow-moving waters, mostly in ponds or lakes.

(For explanations of **larva**, **nymph** and **moult**, see the *Insect* section on p.10..)

## Gastropod mollusc

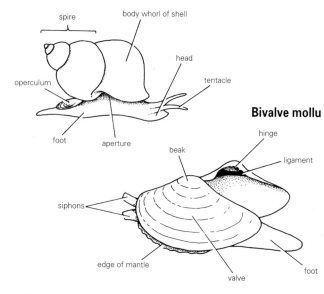

### Bivalve mollu

# Crustacean
(e.g. crayfish)

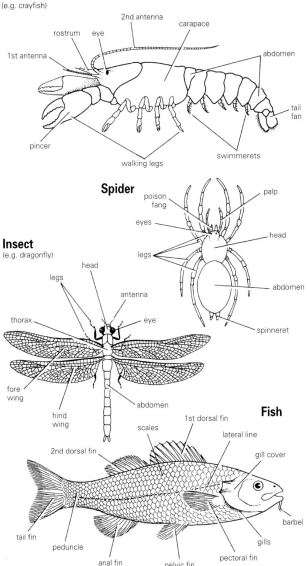

2nd antenna

carapace

rostrum    eye

1st antenna

abdomen

pincer

tail fan

walking legs

swimmerets

# Spider

poison fang

palp

eyes

head

# Insect
(e.g. dragonfly)

legs

head

antenna

legs

eye

thorax

abdomen

fore wing

spinneret

hind wing

abdomen

# Fish

1st dorsal fin

lateral line

scales

gill cover

2nd dorsal fin

barbel

tail fin

gills

peduncle

anal fin

pelvic fin

pectoral fin

# WATER SNAKE
usually up to **70cm**

*Natrix maura*

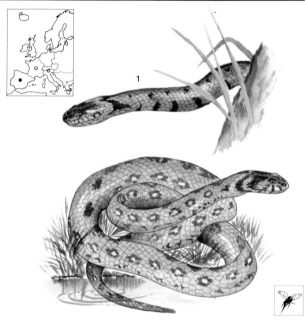

Quite thick-bodied snake, usually grey or brown; may be tinged red or yellow. Black blotches on back and flanks may merge to form cross-bars or zigzags; blotches on flanks are often white-centred. Usually one or two ∧-shaped marks on head.

Active by day. May bask beside water but usually dives if disturbed. Hisses and strikes if cornered but not poisonous. Exudes smelly contents of anal glands if handled. Hunts for fishes and amphibians. Females lay eggs in summer, on land.

Found in or near weedy ponds, streams and rivers, in damp woods and meadows, also in brackish water, up to 1400m in the south of its range. Iberia and France, northwestern Italy and southwestern Switzwerland. Also Balearic Islands and Sardinia.

The related **Grass Snake** *N. natrix* (**1**) is found across most of Europe and British Isles, usually in damp places, often near water (especially in south), but is more terrestrial than Water Snake. Balkan Dice Snake spends much of its life in water.

1

Carapace flattened, more or less oval in outline. Carapace and body dark brown or blackish, usually with yellow spots and streaks. Young are more brightly coloured than adults.

Active by day, hiding in thick vegetation in the water or basking on the bank, ready to dive at any disturbance. A carnivore, hunting invertebrates, fishes and amphibians. Female lays 4-10 eggs in hole in the bank in summer.

Found in slow-moving rivers and stagnant ponds, ditches and marshes, also in brackish water; across southern and much of central Europe. Absent from much of northern France, the British Isles and northern Europe.

**Stripe-necked Terrapin** *Mauremys caspica* (**1**) lives in similar places, also in more open water, in Iberia and southern Balkans. It has a lighter-coloured carapace and yellow stripes on the neck. Tortoises are terrestrial and have a domed carapace.

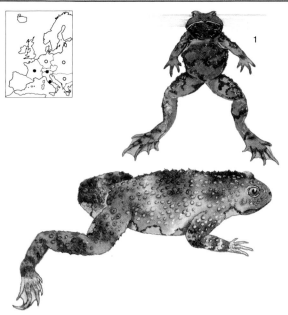

A small warty, aquatic toad; its characteristic yellow belly has dark markings. Colour of back varies from brown or grey to yellowish or olive, the warts often ending in black spiny points.

Mostly active by day. Many are often found together, calling to each other. A toad may turn on its back and exude a distasteful secretion from its skin if threatened. They breed in spring, females laying eggs in the water, in small groups on weeds.

Found in shallow water at edges of rivers and streams, ponds and ditches in lowland and hilly areas. Across most of central and southern Europe, from the French coast eastwards. Absent from Iberia, southern Greece and most Mediterranean Islands.

**Fire-bellied Toad** *B. bombina* (1) is very similar but has a red belly with black markings and its warts are not spiny. It lives in shallow lowland ponds, rivers and ditches from eastern Europe west to Denmark and southern Sweden, south to Hungary and Rumania.

18

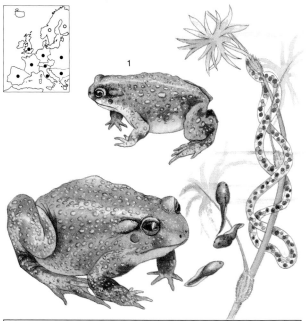

Largest toad in Europe, with warty skin and fairly uniform, sometimes blotchy colour. Usually brownish (sandy brown to redbrown), with lighter, sometimes marbled belly. Eyes deep yellow or copper. Parotoid glands slightly oblique (not parallel).

Hides by day, emerging at dusk to croak, and feed on worms, slugs and insects. Usually walks, but hops if threatened. Returns to shallow ponds in the spring to breed. Male clasps the female while she lays her eggs in strings of toadspawn.

Found on dry land for much of the year, hiding in a variety of places. Occurs throughout most of Europe and Great Britain; one of the commonest European amphibians. Absent from Ireland and many of the Mediterranean Islands.

**Natterjack Toad** *B. calamita* (**1**) is about half the size, has yellow stripe on its back and parallel parotoid glands. Eyes silver-gold. Occurs from Iberia to southern Scandinavia, locally in British Isles, usually in sandy areas & heaths in north of its range.

**Green Toad** *Bufo viridis* (**1**) Up to 10cm long. Warty toad with greenish markings. Mainly nocturnal. Found in dry, often sandy, lowland places, in towns in south of its range. Eastern Europe to Germany, north to Sweden & south to Greece, Italy & Balearic islands. Visits slow streams & ponds in spring, to breed.

**Spadefoot Toad** *Pelobates fuscus* (**2**) Up to 8cm long. Plump, smooth-skinned toad, with flat, sharp-edged 'spade' on each hind foot. Eyes golden with vertical pupils. Varies in colour but often smells of garlic.

Nocturnal. Lives in burrows in sandy ground for most of year; visits deep pools to breed in spring. Central & eastern Europe.

**Parsley Frog** *Pelodytes punctatus* (**3**) Up to 5cm long. Small, agile toad (not a frog) with warty skin, pale grey or olive with darker green markings. Often smells of garlic. Nocturnal. Found in damp places, among bushes, near water; by day under a stone or in a burrow. Returns to still water to breed in late winter & spring. Iberia to France & western Belgium, also northern Italy.

# COMMON FROG

*Rana temporaria*

**6-10cm**

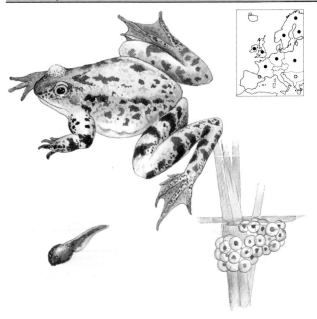

Smooth-skinned frog with relatively blunt snout and ridges of skin along its sides. Grey to brown or olive, with darker blotches, often with dark Λ-shaped mark between shoulders. Breeding males have a dark nuptial pad on thumb.

Active by night; moves on land by leaping, a powerful swimmer in water. Feeds on insects, slugs. Hibernates in mud, soil or water in winter, returning to water to breed in spring. Male clasps female while she lays her eggs in masses of frogspawn.

Lives in a wide variety of moist places, woods, gardens, marshes; also in water, ponds, canals and ditches. The most widespread European frog. Found across much of Europe, but absent from the Balkans, much of Italy and Iberia.

One of several frogs known as Brown Frogs. The very similar **Moor Frog** (p.22) has a more pointed snout, its markings often form stripes, and it has a large, hard tubercle on the hind foot (Common Frog has a small, soft one).

## Brown Frogs

Several species found in Europe (including **Common Frog** - see p.21). They are relatively terrestrial in habits & can croak only quietly. Many have a dark mask across the eyes.

**Moor Frog** *R. arvalis* (**1**) grows up to 8cm long. Similar to Common Frog, but with a more pointed snout; back often striped. Horny tubercle on hind foot is larger & harder than Common Frog's, sometimes sharp-edged. Found in damp places, fields, marshes, bogs & fens, often breeding in temporary pools. Northeast France, east across Europe & north to Sweden. Absent from British Isles & southern Europe.

**Agile Frog** *R. dalmatina* (**2**) grows up to 9cm long. Related to Moor Frog, but not as variable. Usually brown with scattered black spots on the back & strongly banded legs. Groin often yellow. A very agile frog found in damp woods, wet meadows, across Europe. Absent from the British Isles, Iberia & northern Europe.

# OTHER FROGS

*Rana & Hyla* species

**GREEN FROGS**
Related to Brown Frogs but with no dark mask across eyes. Aquatic, often gregarious & noisy, singing by day in & around ponds, ditches, rivers.

**Marsh Frog** *R. ridibunda* (**1**) is the largest European frog, up to 15cm long. Browny-green with dark spots on back, marbled greyish thighs. Vocal sac grey. Iberia & S. France; & from Germany east to Russia & south to Balkans. Introduced to S. Britain & Italy.

**Edible Frog** *R. esculenta* (**2**) grows up to 12cm long. Smaller than Marsh Frog; thighs marbled in yellow & brown, vocal sacs whitish. Italy & S. France, north & east to S. Sweden & Russia.

**TREE FROGS**
Small, plump frogs with long legs; disc-like pads on toes.

**Common Tree Frog** *H. arborea* (**3**) grows 4-5cm long; usually bright green, with dark stripe across eye & along flank. Lives in dense vegetation & reed beds, often high up, but also descending to ponds to breed in spring. Mostly nocturnal, males calling stridently in spring. Throughout much of Europe but absent from north, British Isles & parts of Iberia.

23

# GREAT CRESTED NEWT
**12-14cm**, including tail       *Triturus cristatus*

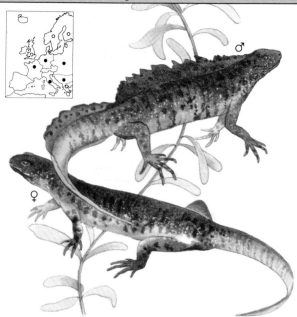

A large, dark newt with coarse skin. Usually dark brown or grey, with yellow or orange belly and dark spots or blotches all over. Breeding males have a high spiky crest on the body and another on the tail; and a bluish stripe on the tail.

Found in and around ponds or slow-moving water throughout the year, on land hiding under stones or logs. They feed on worms, snails and insects. Produce foul-smelling secretion when handled. Females lay single eggs in water in spring.

Found across much of Europe north to central Scandinavia, in the lowlands in the north but at altitudes up to 2000m in the south of its range. Rare now in Great Britain. Absent from Ireland, southern France, Iberia and the Mediterranean Islands.

Marbled Newt is bright, marbled green with a mottled back and white greyish belly. It is found in similar, but more terrestrial, places to the Great Crested Newt, but only in Iberia, southern and western France.

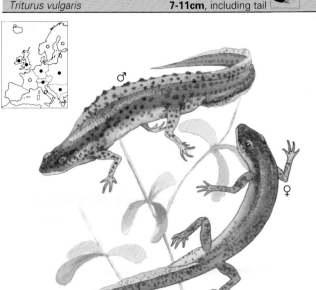

Small newt with smooth skin, often with dark spots on belly and throat, and dark lines through eyes. Three grooves on top of head. Back yellow brown or olive, belly orange. Breeding males have dark spots all over and a crest on tail and body.

Most common newt over much of its range, spending much of the year in damp places on land, under stones, in crevices or logs, in woods, gardens, hedges etc. Comes to shallow, weedy ponds and ditches to breed in spring. Female lays single eggs.

Usually a lowland species especially in the north of its range, but occurs up to 1000m high in the south. Found across much of Europe as far north as central Scandinavia. Absent from Iberia, southern France, southern Italy and the Mediterranean Islands.

**Palmate Newt** (p.26) has much more delicate colouring and no spots on its often pinkish throat. **Alpine Newt** (p.26) has a uniform deep yellow or red belly, generally with no spots.

**Palmate Newt** *T. helveticus* (**1**)
Up to 9cm long (including tail).
Small newt with smooth skin,
olive or pale brown above;
belly with central pale yellow
or silver-orange stripe, often
unspotted or with a few small
spots. Throat always unspotted,
often pinkish. Breeding males
have low crest on back & tail;
tail has orange stripe on the
side, bordered by dark spots.
Found in & near ponds & pools,
often in hills & moors or
mountains. Great Britain &
western Europe, south to N.
Spain & north throughout
Germany. Absent from Ireland.

**Alpine Newt** *T. alpestris* (**2**)
Up to 12cm long (including
tail). Dark brown or grey back
& deep yellow to red, unspotted
belly. Flanks often lighter in
colour (especially in males)
with numerous dark spots.
Breeding males have low,
smooth crest with many dark
spots. Found in or near cold
deep pools or slow-moving
water, usually in mountains,
especially in the south of its
range, but also in cool lowland
ponds in the north. From
Denmark south to N. Italy, east
to Greece & west to French coast.
Also in mountains of N. Spain.

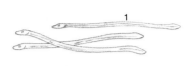

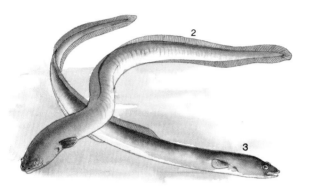

A slimy, cylindrical fish with dorsal, anal and tail fins joined together. Lower jaw longer than upper jaw. Pectoral fins small and rounded, pelvic fins absent. Dorsal fin originates far behind the pectorals. Scales minute and embedded in skin.

Young eels (elvers) live around Atlantic coasts. They change to yellow eels when about 8cm long and swim into rivers, to live in rivers, streams, ditches, ponds and lakes. After several years they change into silver eels and return to sea to spawn.

Yellow eels lie in the mud of coastal waters, estuaries, rivers and lakes during the day, feeding by night on molluscs, crustaceans, insects and other fishes. Silver eels do not feed. Both silver eels and yellow eels are commercially important.

**Elvers** (**1**) are small and transparent, up to 7cm long. **Yellow eels** (**2**) have dark backs and yellow bellies; males grow up to 40cm, females up to 60cm. **Silver eels** (**3**) have even darker backs and larger eyes, their sides and bellies are silver.

# ALLIS SHAD
**30-60cm**

*Alosa alosa*

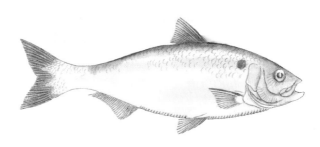

A deep-bodied fish, rather flattened from side to side, with a large head and fragile silvery scales. It has a blue back and silvery sides, both with a metallic gleam. There is usually a black spot behind the gill cover. Upper jaw is notched.

Mature fish migrate into rivers from the sea in spring, going far upriver to spawn, then returning to the sea. Young spend 12 years in rivers before migrating to sea. Young feed on insect larvae and crustaceans; adults only feed in the sea.

Adult Shad live in the Mediterranean, Atlantic and North Sea and at one time spawned in rivers around the whole of this coastline. Northern populations are much reduced by pollution, river locks and weirs. They have little commercial importance.

Twaite Shad are similar but have golden flanks with six or seven spots. They also live in the sea but only migrate into river mouths (to the limit of the tidal influence) to spawn, not far upstream like Allis Shad.

# COMMON WHITEFISH
*Coregonus lavaretus*

**20-45cm**

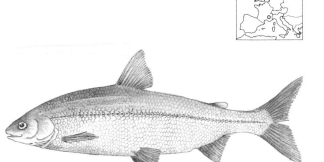

Silver-brown or grey fish with dark back and fins. Small head, a rather flattened, quite deep body, single dorsal fin and a fleshy fin near the deeply forked tail. Mouth lacks teeth. Scales large. An obvious lateral line runs down each side.

Found in clear, well-oxygenated lakes, near the bottom by day, rising to feed at dusk. They eat plankton and insect larvae. Introduced in some lakes. In others, their numbers have been reduced by pollution and competition from introduced species.

Northern Europe, from Norway and Denmark east across Asia. Also in Loch Lomond and Loch Eck in Scotland (where it is known as the Powan), in the English Lake District (where it is known as the Skelly), and in Wales. An important commercial fish.

One of several Whitefish found in Europe. The similar but smaller Cisco or Vendace is found in cold deep lakes and rivers in much of northern Europe, also in Scotland and the Lake District. It grows up to 25cm and has a curved lower jaw.

# GRAYLING
**25-45cm**

*Thymallus thymallus*

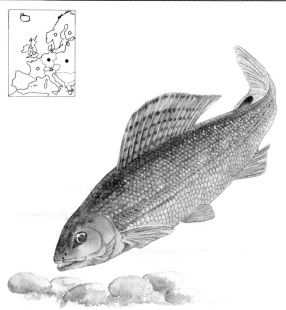

Silvery grey fish with with dark fins, large scales, violet stripes on the sides and an extra fleshy fin on the back near the tail. Dorsal fin is large and high, with a long base, formed of branched rays, and edged with red in males.

Found in small shoals in clean, well-oxygenated water, in fastrunning rivers, also in mountain lakes, usually where there is a good growth of weeds and a sandy or gravelly bottom. They feed on a wide variety of insects and crustaceans.

Found from central France (north of the Alps) east across Europe and Asia; north to Sweden and the Arctic. Also in England and southern Scotland, north and east from the Thames. A good angling fish but now relatively rare due to pollution.

No similar species but its relationship to **Salmon** (opposite) and **Trout** (p.32) can be seen from the fleshy adipose fin near the tail.

# SALMON

*Salmo salar*  usually **50-100cm; 3-10kg**

Large fish with fleshy adipose fin behind dorsal fin. Silvery, with brown-tinged, mottled back and many dark round and xshaped spots. Tail peduncle narrow. 10-13 scales between adipose fin and lateral line. Breeding fish lose their sheen.

Adults live in the sea but enter rivers to spawn far upstream in winter; at this time males have pinkish bellies and strongly hooked jaws. Young salmon swim to the sea when 1-3 years old, returning to spawn for the first time 1-4 years later.

Found in clean, well-oxygenated rivers in the British Isles and Europe, from Iceland and Scandinavia south to northern Spain. Salmon fishing and fish-farming is a major industry, but they are extinct in many rivers, mainly due to dams and pollution.

Young river salmon, or **parr (1)** have dark spots on their backs and a series of dark vertical bars on the sides. They turn silver and are known as smolts when they swim to the sea. **Charr** (p.33) are darker, with pale spots.

31

# BROWN TROUT
**40-50cm**

*Salmo trutta fario*

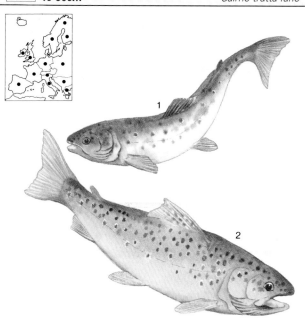

Brown Trout may be long and slim or short and thickset, silvery to almost black, with few to many dark spots. Fleshy adipose fin behind dorsal fin, usually orange-tipped. Tail peduncle deep. 13-16 scales between adipose fin and lateral line.

Found in clean, well-oxygenated waters of lakes, or hiding under the banks and in the pools of streams and rivers, feeding in the shallow waters on insects, crustaceans and other fishes. They do not migrate to the sea.

From the estuaries of lowland rivers and lakes to mountain streams. British Isles and Europe from northern Norway to Spain, east to the Caspian Sea. Important food fishes, both commercially and for anglers. They command high prices.

Larger, more silvery fish (**1**) live mostly in lakes, smaller darker ones (**2**) in streams and rivers. Sea Trout are silvery; adults live in the sea but migrate into lakes and rivers to spawn in winter. **Rainbow Trout** (opposite) have a pink band on each side.

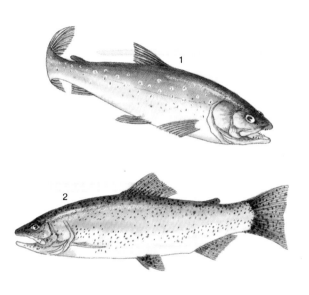

**Charr** *Salvelinus alpinus* (**1**)
Trout-like fish, varying in colour
with locality but usually with
pale spots. Scales minute. Found
in Ireland, Scotland & from
Scandinavia across northern
Europe to Asia & all around the
N. Pole. Some populations do
not migrate to the sea, but live in
clear, often cold lakes. They are
generally smaller (up to 40cm
long) than other European
populations which behave like
salmon, living in the sea and
migrating into large rivers to
spawn. These grow up to 80cm
long. The searun fish are becoming
commercially important.

**Rainbow Trout** *Oncorhynchus
mykiss* (**2**) Usually 25-45cm.
Similar to **Brown Trout**
(opposite) but with an
iridescent pink or red band
running along each flank (the
rainbow) & many black spots.
Introduced from N. America as
sporting fish & for fish farms;
now found in lakes & rivers all
over the British Isles & Europe
& commercially important.

# BREAM OR BRONZE BREAM
usually **30-50cm**

*Abramis brama*

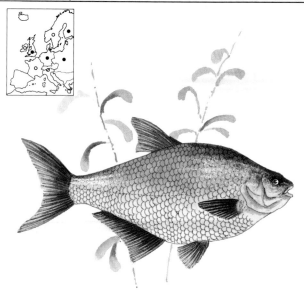

Very deep-bodied, laterally compressed, hump-backed, slimy fish.
Mouth small with thick lips. Eyes small. Anal fin long and concave
in outline, originating beneath dorsal fin. Back and fins brown,
sides and belly silvery with bronze sheen.

Found in shoals in warm, slow-moving or still waters of lowland
rivers, canals and lakes. They live in shallow water among weeds
close to the shore in summer, feeding on bottom-living worms,
insect larvae and molluscs. In deeper water in winter.

From British Isles (including Ireland but not northern Scotland)
east to Russia. North to much of Sweden and Finland, south to the
Alps. Absent from the Mediterranean countries. A good angling
fish. Caught commercially in eastern Europe.

Blue Bream is less deep-bodied, smaller (usually 25-30cm long),
with a brownish or greenish back and yellow sides. It lives in
slow-moving, lowland rivers and lakes in central and eastern
Europe, also in the southern tip of Sweden.

# SILVER BREAM

*Blicca bjoerkna*

usually **20-30cm**

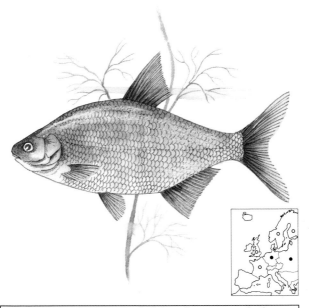

Deep-bodied, rather hump-backed, laterally compressed, silvery fish, darker on its back. It has large eyes, a small mouth and no barbels. The anal fin is long-based and concave in outline, and it originates behind the high dorsal fin.

Lives in warm, slow-moving lowland waters of rivers, canals and lakes, usually in shallow water among weeds. In deeper water in winter. Feeds on bottom-living crustaceans, insect larvae, molluscs and plants in summer, fasting in winter.

Found from southeastern and eastern England, across central Europe to Russia, as far north as southern Sweden and Finland, south to the Alps and Caucasus mountains. It is too small and bony to be commercially important or of interest to anglers.

Silver Bream and young **Bronze Bream** (opposite) are similar; Silver Bream has much larger eyes and larger scales. Anal fin of Bronze Bream originates beneath the dorsal fin. Bronze Bream are more common.

# BLEAK
usually up to **15cm**

*Alburnus alburnus*

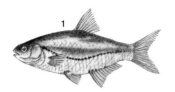

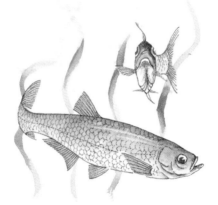

Small, slim, silvery fish with blue-green back and grey fins. Lower lip protrudes beyond upper. Anal fin long, originating beneath the rear of the dorsal fin. Belly keeled between pelvic fins and anal fin. Scales large, shiny and easy to detach.

Lives in large shoals near the surface of clean, slow-moving or still waters, in lowland rivers and lakes. They can be seen rising to the surface on warm summer days to catch flies and other insects. Found in deeper water in winter.

Found in most parts of England and eastern Wales; and across Europe to the Caspian Sea. North to much of Sweden and Finland, south to the Alps. Absent from most Mediterranean countries. An important food fish for other species like pike and perch.

**Schneider** *Alburnoides bipunctatus* (**1**) is similar but smaller (10-12cm long) with a dark stripe along each side. It lives in similar places to Bleak, from western France across central Europe, eastward to Russia.

# ORFE OR IDE

*Leuciscus idus*

usually **30-45cm**

Relatively thick-set fish with a hump behind the head, a broad snout and downturned mouth. Back grey to black, sides and belly silvery. Fins red-tinged, except dorsal fin. Anal fin straightedged or concave. 55-61 scales along lateral line.

Lives in clean, slow-flowing lowland rivers and lakes, in deeper water in winter. Feeds on insects and their larvae, crustaceans and molluscs.

Found in Europe from eastern France north to the Baltic (where it is found in brackish water) and Sweden, and east to Siberia. Absent from southern Europe. Introduced to southern England. Caught commercially in eastern Europe and a good angling fish.

**Roach** (p.38) has a deeper body and 42-45 scales in the lateral line. Golden Orfe is a variety of Orfe often seen in ornamental ponds; it has a golden sheen.

# ROACH
usually **20-35cm**

*Rutilus rutilus*

A relatively deep-bodied, laterally compressed fish with large silvery scales. Mouth small. Back bluish or brownish, shading to silver-brown or green-gold on the sides, belly silvery. Fins red-brown; dorsal fin originates above the pelvic fins.

Lives in shoals, common in lowland areas, from small ponds to large lakes, streams and rivers, canals, often where there are dense weeds so they can hide from pike. Feed on insect larvae, crustaceans, molluscs and water weeds.

Found from Ireland across Europe to Asia, north to much of Sweden and Finland, south to the Alps. Mostly absent from the Mediterranean countries. Caught commercially in eastern Europe; a popular angling fish in Britain.

Several other Roach species occur in Europe (the Adriatic Roach in rivers running into the Adriatic, and the Pardillo Roach in Portugal and Spain). In **Rudd** (opposite), the dorsal fin originates behind the pelvic fins.

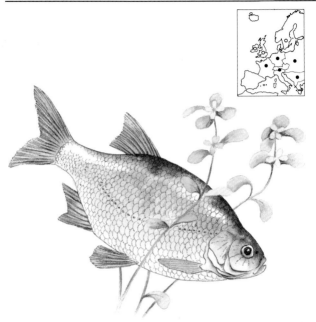
*Scardinius erythrophthalmus*          usually **20-30cm**

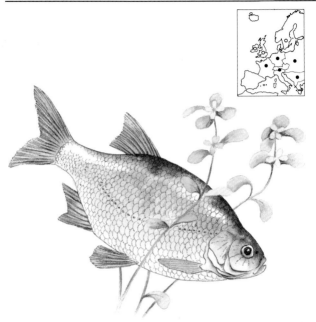

A deep-bodied, quite laterally compressed fish, larger ones hump-backed. Scales large, silvery and firmly attached. Mouth upturned. Back usually brownish green, sides brassy and belly whitish. Fins red; dorsal fin originates behind pelvic fins.

Lives in dense shoals in lowland lakes and the slow-moving lower reaches of rivers, usually where there is a rich growth of weeds. Feeds on insects and their larvae, crustaceans, also plants. They often carry **Fish Lice** (p.67).

Found locally from Ireland and Great Britain (except Scotland) east across Europe to Asia; north to southern Sweden and south to the Mediterranean. Absent from Iberia. Fished commercially in eastern Europe and a popular angling fish in Britain.

In the similar **Roach** (opposite), the dorsal fin originates above the pelvic fins and the mouth is not upturned.

A relatively slim fish with a small head and mouth. Dorsal and anal fins are concave; dorsal fin originates above the pelvic fins. Body is silvery with a bluish back and large silvery scales. Pectoral, pelvic and anal fins are flushed with orange.

Lives in shoals near the surface, usually in clear, fastflowing middle reaches of lowland rivers and streams, less often in slow-flowing lower reaches and lakes. Feeds on plants, insects and their larvae, molluscs and crustaceans.

Found in southern Ireland, England, Wales and southern Scotland. Across Europe to Asia, north throughout Sweden and Finland. Absent from Iberia, most of Italy and Greece. Popular angling fish but they compete with salmon in salmon streams.

The anal fins of **Chub** (opposite) are convex in outline. **Rudd** (p.39) are deeper bodied and their dorsal fin originates well behind the pelvic fin.

*Leuciscus cephalus*  usually **30-50cm**

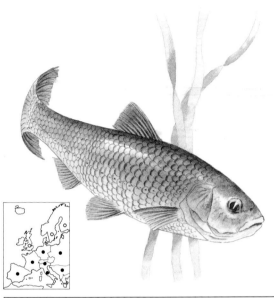

Elongated but round-bodied fish with blunt head. Mouth large. Scales large, dark-edged. Dorsal and anal fins square-cut or convex. Back dark green-grey, sides metallic blue or silvery, belly silver-yellow. Pelvic and anal fins yellow or reddish.

Found in middle reaches of clean rivers, where shallows and pools alternate, basking in shallow water in summer, hiding in pools in winter. Feed on insect larvae and small fish. Young fish live in small shoals, older ones are more solitary.

Found in lowland areas of England, and across lowland Europe to the Caspian Sea. They are found north to southern Sweden and south to the Mediterranean. The Chub is a popular angling fish but not good to eat.

**Dace** (opposite) have concave edges to the anal fin. Grass Carp have been introduced in many ponds and canals to control weeds; and they are popular angling fish; in the water they may look like golden Chub.

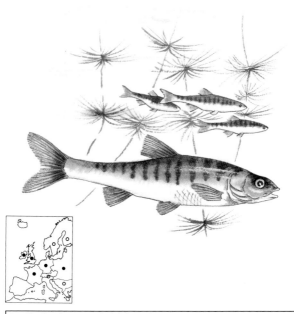

Small, slim but rounded fish with tiny scales. Lateral line ends in region of anal fin. Colour varies, usually green-brown back with yellow-white belly and irregular dark stripes on each side. Breeding male has red belly (in early summer).

Very common in clean flowing upland rivers or the smaller lowland streams, sometimes in lakes; forming shoals near the surface of the water in summer. They hide beneath stones in winter. Feed on tiny crustaceans, insect larvae and algae.

Found from Ireland and Britain (except northern Scotland) across Europe to Asia, north to Sweden and Finland. Absent from Iberia, most of Italy and Greece. Commercially unimportant but popular with children for catching in jam-jars.

**Bitterling** (opposite) has no stripes on its sides; does have a blue streak near the tail. **Sticklebacks** (pp.59 & 61) have spines on their backs. **Gudgeon** (p.45) and **Stone Loach** (p.50) have barbels.

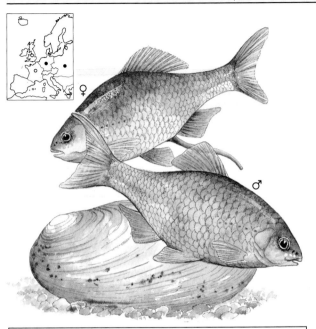
*Rhodeus sericeus*

usually **5-7cm**

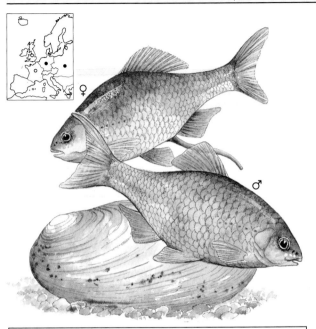

♀

♂

Small, deep-bodied, laterally compressed fish. Lateral line short, ending over pectoral fins. Back grey-green, sides and belly silver-white, with metallic blue-green streak near tail; fins tinged orange. Colours of breeding males very bright.

Found in weedy, slow-moving rivers, canals, ponds and lakes where the bottom is silty sand. Feed on small invertebrates and algae. Females lay eggs in **Freshwater Mussels** (p.110), using the long egg-tube. Males set up territories around the mussels.

Found across central Europe from northern France eastwards to Asia. Introduced to a few ponds in northern England and spreading southwards. Absent from Scandinavia and southern Europe. No commercial importance.

No other species behaves like this: the breeding habits of this fish are unique. **Minnow** (opposite) has dark stripes on its sides.

43

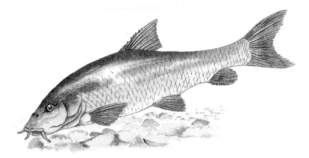

Long, slim fish with a rounded body. Four barbels; two on the pointed snout and two in the jaw angles. Single dorsal fin has a short base and three spines, one of them stout and serrated. Brownish green head and back, golden brown sides, creamy belly.

Found in lowland reaches of fast-flowing, relatively deep rivers over sand or gravel, often in the deeper pools, near weirs or bridges. They rest by day, feeding mostly at night on bottom-living insect larvae, crustaceans, worms and molluscs.

Occurs across Europe from England and France to the Black Sea, absent from the south and north. A good angling fish.

One of several barbels found in Europe, including the Mediterranean Barbel from southern Europe; it has dark spots on its back. Small Barbels may be mistaken for **Gudgeon** (opposite), but the latter have only two barbels.

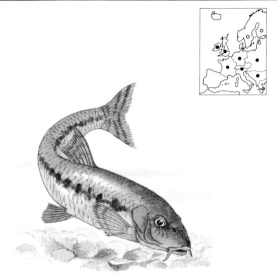

A small, slender fish with a long body, heavy head and two barbels, one at each corner of the mouth. It is silvery, darker on the back than the belly, with a row of dark spots on each side. Its single dorsal fin has a short base.

Found in large shoals, most often in clean, fast-flowing lowland streams and rivers, usually near the bottom over clean sand or gravel, less often in lakes. It feeds on insects, crustaceans and molluscs.

Found from the British Isles (absent from northern Scotland) eastwards across central Europe to Asia (north to southern Sweden and south to the south of France and the northern Baltic). Commercially unimportant but used for angling bait.

Several other gudgeon species live in Europe; all are small fishes with two barbels. Small **Barbels** (opposite) have four barbels around the mouth. **Stone Loach** (p.50) may be found in similar places but have six barbels.

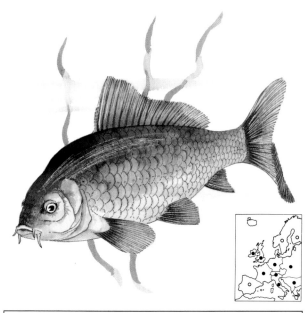

Large, rather elongated, deep-bodied fish with large rounded scales. Four barbels on upper lip. Dorsal fin dark, with long base and toothed spine at front end. Colour varies but back usually brown to brownish green, shading to a yellowish belly.

Found singly or in small shoals among dense weeds, in slowmoving, lowland rivers, lakes and ponds. Feeds on crustaceans, insect larvae and molluscs in summer, often stirring up the mud at the bottom; in winter they often stop feeding.

Throughout Europe (except far north); introduced to England, Wales and Ireland. Important commercial and popular angling fish, introduced to many ponds and lakes since it grows fast, but causing environmental problems in the way it feeds.

Koi and Mirror Carp are ornamental forms of the Common Carp (Koi are multicoloured and Mirror Carp have only a few large scales, the 'mirrors').

# CRUCIAN CARP

*Carassius carassius*  usually **10-30cm**

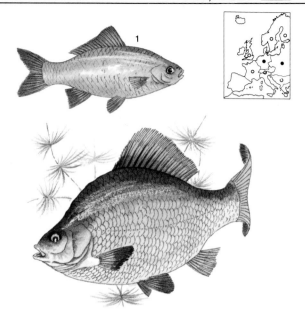

Very deep-bodied, hump-backed fish with relatively large, rounded scales. Single long dorsal fin has three spiny rays at the front; the third spine is slightly serrated. Usually olive brown or olive green, with paler, brassy sides.

Found in still, lowland waters, marshes, weedy lakes and ponds, backwaters of slow-moving rivers, where it is able to tolerate the poorly oxygenated water. Feeds on insect larvae, crustaceans and molluscs, also on water plants.

Native from southeast England and eastern France north to Sweden and east to Asia; introduced elsewhere in Europe. Absent from Spain, most of Italy and Greece. Valuable commercial fish in eastern Europe. Also a popular ornamental and angling fish.

The related but slimmer **Goldfish** *C. auratus* (**1**) have been introduced as ornamental fishes to many ponds and lakes in Europe and the British Isles; they come from Asia.

# TENCH
usually **20-40cm**

*Tinca tinca*

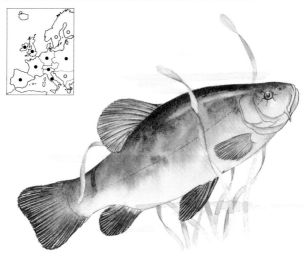

A heavy, deep-bodied, very slimy fish with small scales deeply embedded in the skin. It has two barbels, one at each corner of the mouth. Colour varies with habitat, usually dark green with a bronze sheen and bronze belly. Fins dark and rounded.

A secretive fish, found in still (even stagnant) or very slowmoving, lowland waters, where the bottom is muddy, among dense weeds. They feed on bottom-living worms, molluscs, crustaceans and insects, also on plants.

Found across Europe from the British Isles east to Asia but absent from the north (including northern Scotland and most of Scandinavia). Commercially not important but a good angling fish and used to stock small, oxygen-deficient ponds.

Golden Tench are kept in ornamental ponds.

48

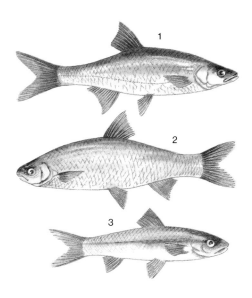

**Asp** *Aspius aspius* (**1**)
Usually 40-60cm. Slim fish with large mouth. Lower jaw has tubercle at its tip which fits into notch on upper jaw. Back dark green, sides & belly silvery, fins tinged with red. Solitary fish, found in middle reaches of rivers & lakes, in deep pools, under banks. Holland & S. Sweden east to Russia. Commercially important in eastern Europe.

**Nase** *Chondrostoma nasus* (**2**)
Usually 20-40cm. Slim fish with protruding snout & sharp lower lip. Grey with yellowish belly; lower fins orange, dorsal & tail

fin reddish. Large shoals live in pools of fast-flowing rivers, often in upper reaches. Across central Europe from France to Caspian Sea. French Nase *C. toxostoma* (not illustrated) is smaller (20-25cm), with yellowish fins. Lives in upper reaches of rivers & streams, in W. France, N. Spain & Portugal.

**Souffie** *Leuciscus souffia* (**3**)
Usually 10-12cm. Slim-bodied fish with dark stripe on each side; lateral line & fin bases orange. Lives in large shoals in running water over gravel, in upper reaches of Danube & Rhine, S. France & N. Italy.

# STONE LOACH
usually **8-12cm**        *Noemacheilus barbatulus*

A small, elongated, scaleless fish with rounded fins. The mouth is on the underside of the snout; there are six conspicuous barbels around the mouth. This fish is variable in colour, usually dull yellow-brown with dark brown markings.

Lives on the bottom, hiding under stones and among dense water weeds, in the clean running water of small streams; also around the shores of lakes and in lagoons in the Baltic. Feeds on bottom-living insect larvae, crustaceans, worms and molluscs.

Found in the British Isles (except northern Scotland) and from western Europe across Asia. North to southern Sweden and Finland; south to eastern Spain, northern Italy and northern Greece. A food fish for for trout and other fishes.

**Spined Loach** (opposite) has a spine beneath each eye and shorter barbels; it also has lines of dark spots along each flank.

# SPINED LOACH

*Cobitis taenia*                                    usually 5-12cm

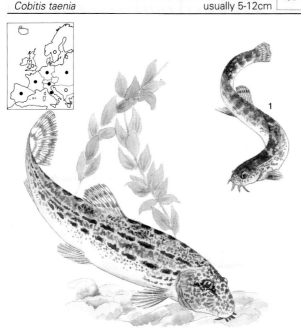

A small, elongated, scaleless fish with rounded fins and six short barbels around the mouth. There is a double spine below each eye. Its back is marbled brown in colour, with a row of dark spots running along each flank; belly yellow-white.

Hides for much of the time in sand or mud at the bottom of still and slow-moving waters of streams and lakes. When active, it feeds on small bottom-living invertebrates. May come up to the surface to gulp air when the water is low in oxygen.

Found from East Anglia in England, across much of Europe. North to southern Sweden, south to the Mediterranean. Thought to be rare but its secretive life style makes its numbers difficult to assess. Sometimes kept as an aquarium fish.

**Weatherfish** *Misgurnus fossilis* (**1**) is a much larger loach (up to 30cm long), with 10 barbels around its mouth. It lives buried in mud in lakes and river backwaters from Holland east across Europe to Asia. This fish gets very restless when a storm is coming.

# WELS OR CATFISH
usually **1-2m; 22-26kg**                    *Silurus glanis*

Very large, heavy fish with a broad head and elongated body.
Mouth is wide with two long barbels on upper jaw, four shorter
ones on lower jaw. Dorsal fin small, anal fin very long. Skin
smooth and slimy, scaleless. Back and head dark, sides marbled.

A solitary fish found in still waters of marshes, lakes, lower reaches
and backwaters of deep rivers, also in lagoons of Baltic Sea. Feeds
on bottom-living invertebrates when young, larger fish catch fish,
frogs, birds and small mammals.

Native to central and eastern Europe, north to southern Sweden
and east to Asia. Introduced to southern England, France and
Germany. Commercially important in eastern Europe. They are
also caught by anglers, putting up a good fight.

Two American Catfishes have been introduced to lakes and
slowmoving rivers in Europe (especially south). They are heavy-
bodied, up to 30cm long, with a smaller mouth than the Wels, an
extra fleshy fin on the back near the tail, and eight barbels.

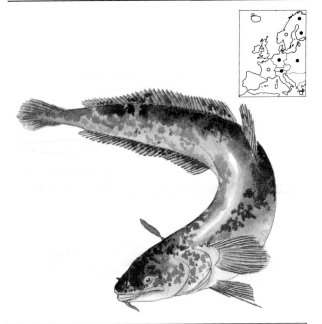

Elongated fish with smooth, slimy skin. Scales very small, embedded in skin. Two dorsal fins; first rounded, second long and narrow like anal fin. One long barbel on the chin. Dull green-brown in colour, mottled with darker markings.

A sluggish fish, hiding by day under rocks, in deep holes or among weeds, emerging by night to feed on crustaceans and other fishes. It lives in clean water in lakes, the lower reaches of rivers, and in brackish lagoons in the Baltic.

Found across the northern hemisphere, including northern Europe, Asia and North America. North into the Arctic and south to the Alps. Probably extinct in England (only ever found in East Anglia). Said to be good to eat.

The only freshwater member of the Cod family in Europe; others are marine. Freshwater fish that resemble it are **Wels** (opposite, with one small dorsal fin and six barbels) and **Eel** (p.27), with one long dorsal fin continuous with tail and anal fin, and no barbel.

53

# PERCH
usually **20-35cm**

*Perca fluviatilis*

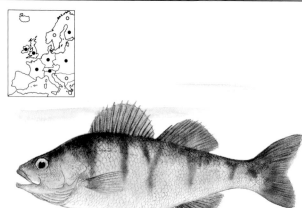

Relatively deep-bodied fish with two dorsal fins, first spiny and longer than non-spiny second. Back dark, sides yellow-white with dark bars; there is a black spot at the back of the first dorsal fin. Anal and pelvic fins are red. Scales rough-edged.

Common in ponds, lakes, canals, slow-moving rivers and streams; smaller ones live in shoals, older fish lurk around bridges, tree roots, reeds and other obstacles. Feed during the day on crustaceans, aquatic insects and their larvae, fish fry.

Found throughout much of Europe and British Isles, east across Asia. Absent from the far north of Scotland and Norway, and from Iberia, southern Italy and the east coast of the Adriatic. A popular angling fish but its spines can inflict nasty cuts.

**Largemouth Bass** (p.60) is a North American fish introduced to lakes and slow-moving rivers in southern England and Europe. It resembles a Perch but has one notched dorsal fin and no red fins. It feels smoother since its scales are not rough-edged.

54

# RUFFE OR POPE

*Gymnocephalus cernuus*    usually **12-20cm**

Small perch-like fish in which the 'two' dorsal fins are joined; the first part of the fin is spiny, the rear part softrayed. Body green-brown with many dark spots, belly lighter, yellowish; there are rows of dark spots on the dorsal fins.

Lives in small shoals in deep, slow-flowing rivers, dykes and canals, also in lakes and in slightly brackish water in the Baltic. Feeds on the bottom, catching insect larvae (especially bloodworms) and small crustaceans.

Found locally in eastern England and across Europe from France to Asia, north to Sweden and Siberia, south to the Alps. Absent from Mediterranean countries. No commercial importance and often a nuisance to anglers, eating the bait.

Small **Pikeperch** (p.56) may resemble Ruffe, but have separate dorsal fins. **Perch** (opposite) also have two dorsal fins and are much more brightly coloured.

55

# PIKEPERCH
usually **40-50cm**

*Stizostedion lucioperca*

Elongated fish, with long, pointed snout and a wide mouth with fang-like teeth. Scales small. Two separate dorsal fins, the first spiny; both fins have rows of dark spots. Green-brown in colour, young fish with indistinct dark bars on the sides.

Lives in larger lakes, canals and rivers, especially over a hard bottom; water may be clear or cloudy. Adults are solitary, aggressive hunters, hunting in open water for other fishes, including roach, bream etc. Young fish feed on invertebrates.

Native to Europe from the Netherlands east to the Caspian Sea, north to southern Sweden and south to the Balkans. Introduced to eastern England, France and Germany. A popular angling fish and good to eat. Caught commercially in eastern Europe.

**Pike** (opposite) has only one dorsal fin set far back on the body near the tail. Young Pikeperch may resemble **Ruffe** (p.55), but in Ruffe the two dorsal fins are joined together.

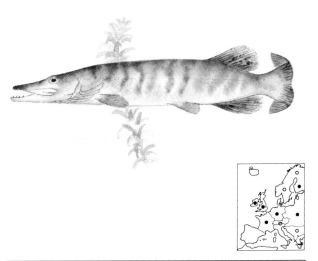

Large fish with elongated but rounded body. Snout almost like a duck's bill. Teeth large and sharp. Dorsal and anal fin near the tail and opposite each other. Colour usually dark green-brown, flecked and barred with cream or yellow. Scales large.

Pike usually hide among water weeds in slow-moving, lowland rivers and lakes. They lie in wait for their prey during the day, catching insect larvae and crustaceans when young, moving on to frogs, then other fishes, ducks and small mammals.

Widespread throughout much of the British Isles and Europe. Absent from northern Scotland, also absent from Iberia, southern Italy, the Balkans and Greece. A favourite angling fish.

The related Amur Pike lives in Siberia. The unrelated **Pikeperch** (opposite) is similar in shape and is also a hunter; it can easily be distinguished from the Pike by its two large dorsal fins.

# MILLER'S THUMB OR BULLHEAD
usually about **10cm**                    *Cottus gobio*

Small fish with a broad, rather flattened head and wide mouth. There is one powerful spine on the front gill cover. Two dorsal fins. Pectoral fins large. Pelvic fins pale in colour. Body scaleless, brown to grey in colour, mottled with dark brown.

Found in shallow, fast-flowing streams, rivers and lakes over a sandy or stony bottom. A solitary fish, usually hiding under a stone. Makes zigzag dashes into cover if disturbed. Feeds on bottom-living crustaceans and insect larvae.

Found in England and Wales and across Europe, from France north to central Scandinavia and Finland, south to northern Spain. Then east to Russia. Absent from southern Italy and Greece. No commercial importance.

Siberian Bullhead is similar; it is found in stony streams and lakes in Scandinavia and Denmark, also in Siberia. Several other bullheads live around the European coasts. **Sticklebacks** (opposite & p.61) have three or nine spines on the back.

# THREE-SPINED STICKLEBACK

*Gasterosteus aculeatus*                    usually **4-8cm**

Small fish with three spines in front of dorsal fin (two large spines and one small one). Pelvic fin consists of one spine and one ray. Colour variable, silvery green to black on the back, silver sides and white belly. Breeding males have red bellies.

Found in weedy lowland ditches and ponds, canals, lakes and rivers; also in estuaries and around the coast. Breeding males make nests in spring and entice females to lay their eggs in them, then guard the young. Feed on a variety of invertebrates.

Common and widespread, even in polluted waters, all over British Isles and western Europe; north to maritime areas of Scandinavia, and south to north coast of Mediterranean. Important food source for birds and other fishes.

**Nine-spined Stickleback** (p.61) has nine or ten spines on the back. **Minnow** (p.42) lacks spines. All these small fishes are the 'tiddlers' caught by children in jam-jars.

**Sturgeon** *Acipenser sturio* (**1**) has five rows of bony plates running along body. Snout long, with two pairs of barbels. Blue-black back, lighter sides, white beneath. Dorsal plates light-coloured, especially in young fish. Once quite common, now rare due to overfishing (eggs are prized as caviar). Adults live in sea but swim into rivers yearly to spawn. Now only found in R. Guadalquivir in Spain R. Gironde in France, & L. Ladoga in Russia. Other more populous species occur in the Danube & rivers running into Black Sea, Caspian Sea & Sea of Azov.

**Largemouth Bass** *Micropterus salmoides* (**2**) Usually 20-40cm. An elongated fish with a large head, a wide mouth & protruding lower jaw. Dorsal fin deeply notched; first part spiny, rear part soft. Back dark olive-green, belly whitish; an irregular dark band runs along each side. Introduced to lakes & slow-moving rivers in southern England & much of Europe from N. America; good angling fish. The related Smallmouth Bass *M. dolomieui* & Pumpkinseed *Lepomis gibbosus* (not illustrated) have also been introduced into Europe from N. America.

**Nine-spined Stickleback**
*Pungitius pungitius* (**1**) Usually
4-7cm long. Very small fish with
8-10 spines on its back. Pelvic
fin consists of one spine & one
ray. Olivegreen to black back,
with dark bars on sides &
silvery belly. Found in still,
shallow, weedy ditches, ponds
& backwaters. Breeding males
make weed nests, entice
females to lay eggs in them,
then guard the young. Found in
lowland areas of E. England &
Ireland, east & north across
Europe from N. France.

**Freshwater Blenny** *Blennius
fluviatilis* (**2**) Usually 8-12cm.
Small fish with elongated body
& very long dorsal fin; anal fin
similar but shorter. Pectoral fins
large; pelvic fins have only two
rays & are placed beneath head.
There is a small growth above
each eye. Body scaleless, rather
slimy, greenish with dark, broken
bars on sides, belly yellowish.
Found in slow-flowing streams
& lakes, & in brackish lagoons,
around the north coast of the
Mediterranean Sea.

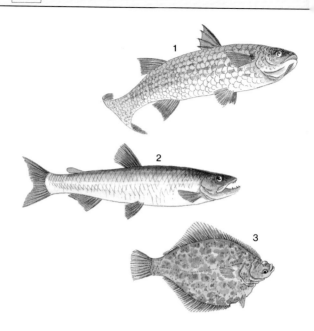

**Thin-lipped Grey Mullet** *Liza ramada* (**1**) 25-40cm long. Dark blue-grey fish with silver sides, striped from head to tail by grey bands. Two dorsal fins & anal fin are all short-based; first dorsal fin has four spines. Mullet swim in shoals, in coastal waters & estuaries in summer, penetrating into fresh water. They withdraw to sea in winter. South & west of British Isles & Mediterranean.

**Smelt** *Osmerus eperlanus* (**2**) Up to 30cm long. Slender fish with an extra fleshy fin on the back near the tail. Light olive green back, a silver stripe along each side, creamy-white belly. Smells of cucumber. Adults live in clean estuaries around Baltic, North Sea & Atlantic south to Bay of Biscay, entering lower reaches of rivers to spawn in spring.

**Flounder** *Platichthys flesus* (**3**) Up to 20-30cm. Only flatfish found in fresh water; many others live in the sea. Found in brackish water & estuaries of Baltic, North Sea, Atlantic & Mediterranean. Young fish are most likely to swim into fresh water sometimes found many km from the sea in lakes & rivers.

# BROOK LAMPREY

*Lampetra planeri*

**14-18cm**

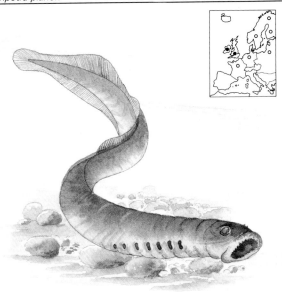

Slimy-skinned, eel-like animal, with no jaws but a small sucking disc around the mouth. Large eyes. Seven gill openings behind the head. Two continuous but distinct dorsal fins. No paired fins. Back grey or brown, becoming paler beneath.

The blind larvae live in rich organic mud in small streams and the upper reaches of rivers. They feed on micro-organisms. After 3-5 years they measure 14-18cm and change into adults during winter. Adults do not feed but spawn in spring and die.

Found locally in the British Isles and northern Europe from France to Scandinavia. No commercial value but used as angling bait.

River Lamprey larvae are similar, but adults grow up to 50cm and have sharp teeth on the sucking disc. They migrate to the sea, feeding parasitically on fishes (such as Salmon) on the way. After several years they return to the rivers to spawn and die.

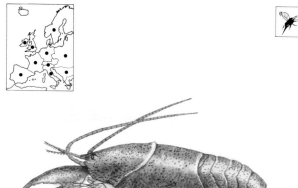

Lobster-like crustacean, head and thorax covered by carapace. Head has two pairs of antennae and eyes on stalks. Thorax bears five pairs of 'walking legs', first pair with large pincers. Abdomen has five pairs of swimmerets and ends in a tail fan.

Crayfish hide under stones by day, searching for food by night. They feed on dead or dying fish, snails and other crustaceans. If disturbed they swim quickly backwards with a flick of the tail fan. Females carry eggs on the swimmerets in winter.

Several species occur in Europe and the British Isles, in lakes, streams and rivers, always in hard water. Their populations have been severely depleted in recent years, by a fungus disease and by acid rain.

**British (white-clawed) Crayfish** (illustrated) has pincers with white undersides; it lives in streams over chalk or limestone, in western Europe, England, Wales and Ireland. European (red-clawed) Crayfish *Astacus astacus* is farmed and also found wild.

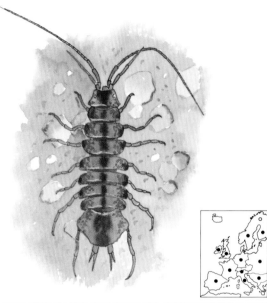

Small, brown, flattened crustaceans, like aquatic woodlice, with a body of many similar segments and seven pairs of legs on the thorax. The head has two pairs of antennae, the outer ones large, the inner ones small, and large eyes.

Abundant wherever there is much decaying plant material on which they feed. They crawl and hide among the plants, under stones and on the muddy bottom. Tolerant of polluted water. Females carry eggs in a brood pouch on the underside in spring.

Several species of water slater are found in Europe and the British Isles, except in the far north. They are often abundant in weedy ponds, around lake margins, in canals and streams. They may be eaten by fish and water birds.

***Asellus aquaticus*** (illustrated) is the most common and the largest, up to 25mm long; its antennae are almost as long as its body. Less common and smaller, *A. meridionalis* has antennae which are only two-thirds as long as the body.

# FRESHWATER SHRIMPS
usually **12-15mm**

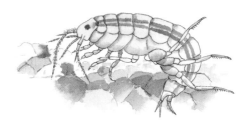

Small, laterally compressed, often curved crustaceans, with large eyes and two pairs of antennae. The body has many similar segments with five pairs of legs on the thorax. Abdomen has three pairs of legs (swimmerets) and ends in a tail fan.

Found on the bottom among stones, around water plants, scuttling for shelter if disturbed. Scavengers, feeding on decaying material. Mating pairs often seen together (males larger); females carry young in a brood pouch in spring.

Several species are found in Europe and the British Isles; and they are very common except in the far north. They may be abundant in both fresh and brackish water, in ponds, ditches, canals, rivers and streams. Fish and water birds feed on them.

Not true shrimps but related to the marine sandhoppers. The native *Gammarus pulex* (illustrated) swim on their sides. *Crangonyx pseudogracilis* (introduced from N. America and now widely distributed in Britain and Europe) swims upright.

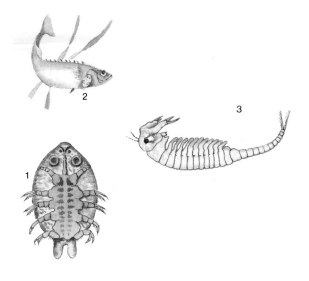

**Fish Louse** *Argulus foliaceus* (**1**) About 5mm long. Parasitic crustacean, found attached to the bodies of many kinds of fish (**2**). It has a flattened, transparent body, with two large suckers near the head; a sharp beak to penetrate the skin just behind the suckers; & four pairs of legs. Also found swimming free, when a fish dies or if the female fish lice are off to lay their eggs on a stone. Several species found in Europe & the British Isles, on Salmon, Grayling, Carp, Perch, & many other fishes.

**Fairy Shrimp** *Chirocephalus diaphanus* (**3**) About 12mm long. Transparent, with many similar segments & leaf-like swimming legs. Head bears two pairs of antennae & large eyes on stalks. Swims on its back, straining small organisms from the water with its legs, passing them to the mouth. Found in temporary ponds, sometimes in large numbers; most common in spring. Females store eggs in the brood pouch; when the pond dries up they die, but the eggs sink into the mud & survive until pond refills again. British Isles & Europe.

# WATER SPIDER
body about **12mm** long      *Argyroneta aquatica*

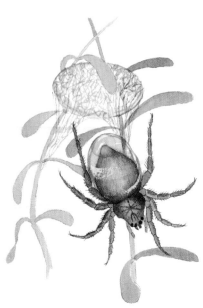

Only truly aquatic spider. Like all spiders it has two parts to the body, the head and abdomen, and eight legs on the head. The head also bears multiple eyes, poison fangs and palps. Silk is spun from the spinners on the abdomen.

It makes an air-filled, bell-like web, attached to underwater plants; carries air from the surface to the bell, as a shining layer trapped by hairs on the abdomen. Hunts underwater for crustaceans, insects and insect larvae, taking them to the bell to eat them.

This is the only spider to live under the surface of the water. Found locally in weedy ponds and lakes, slow-moving ditches and streams. It hibernates in the bell in winter. Throughout the British Isles and Europe, most common in uplands

Many other spiders live around but not under water. **Raft Spider** (opposite) lives on the surface (although it can dive); it is larger, with a yellow or white band on each side of the body.

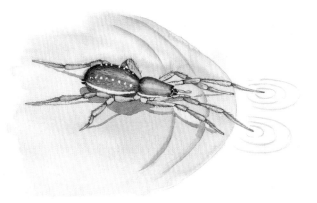

The largest European spider. It has long legs, the two front legs held close together when the spider is at rest. Body brown, with a yellow or white band on each side.

May be seen resting on floating leaves with front legs touching the water, then darting across the water to catch an insect. It may run down the stem of a water plant into the water to avoid danger or to hunt prey. Hunts insects and crustaceans.

Found locally in swamps, marshes and ditches, around pond margins. Found in the south of the British Isles and across Europe, but becoming scattered and rare further north. The bite of this large spider is somewhat poisonous to people.

**Water Spider** (opposite) lives under the surface, in an air-filled, bell-like web. Many other spiders live around ponds, in marshes and other wet places. **Mites** (p.121) are much smaller, with only one round part to the body; many species live in fresh water.

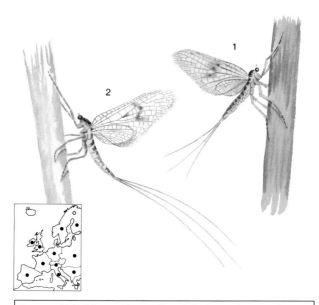

Insects with soft brownish or yellowish bodies and two or three long tail filaments. Most have two pairs of wings, held upright when at rest. Fore wings are large, more or less triangular, with many veins and cross veins. Hind wings smaller or absent.

Mayfly nymphs emerge from water in summer, to moult into immature adults (duns). These moult again within 24 hours into adults (known as spinners); they mate, the females lay their eggs in water, and then they die. Their flight is weak.

Found around fresh water throughout the British Isles and Europe; the males gather in swarms. Mayflies are a favourite food for trout and other fishes. Many of the 'flies' used by fly fishermen are imitations of duns and spinners.

**Duns (1)** have opaque, hairy wings and dull-coloured bodies. **Spinners (2)** have shiny clear wings and bright shiny bodies. The two illustrated are the dun and spinner of **Green Drake**, one of the largest European mayflies.

Elongated, aquatic insects with three pairs of legs on the thorax, and three hairy tail-filaments at the end of the abdomen. Abdomen bears a series of gills, usually projecting from the sides. Wing-buds can be seen on the thorax.

Mostly feed on algae and other water plants. They live in the water for many months, moulting often, growing a little larger after each moult. Finally, in summer, they climb into the air on a plant stem and moult once more, emerging as a 'dun'.

Found in all kinds of fresh water, from fast-flowing streams to big rivers, ponds, lakes and ditches. Throughout Europe and the British Isles.

There are several families of Mayflies, each with a distinct type of nymph, many of them illustrated on this and the next two pages. **Green Drake** nymph (illustrated on this page) is one of the largest, growing up to 25mm long.

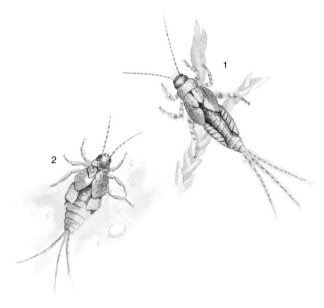

Although relatively similar in appearance, the nymphs of mayflies lead a variety of different life-styles.

**BURROWING NYMPHS** like the nymph of **Green Drake** (illustrated on p.71), burrow into the silt at the bottom of lakes, ponds & rivers. These nymphs have a narrow head with large jaws, & large, feathery gills held over the back of the abdomen.

**CREEPING NYMPHS** The nymphs of **Blue-winged Olive** *Ephemerella ignita* (**1**) & a few related species creep about among the water plants in rivers. They grow about 8mm long & have plate-like gills attached to the back of the abdomen. Their legs & tails are striped in yellow and white. Blue-winged Olive is a common mayfly along rivers, especially where water plants grow thickly.

**Anglers' Curse** nymphs *Caenis* sp. (**2**) are very small (6mm long at most) & have all but the first pair of gills covered by a gill-cover. They are often camouflaged in silt; they live in the silt among the stones of rivers, or around the margins of ponds & lakes.

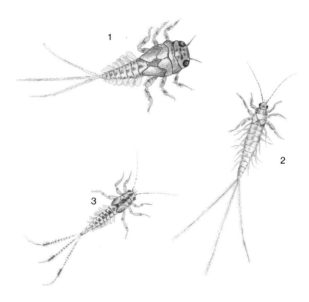

**STONE-CLINGING NYMPHS**
like that of **Autumn Dun**
*Ecdyonurus dispar* (**1**) cling to
the undersides of stones in stony,
fast-flowing rivers & streams, or
in the stony margins of lakes.
They have flattened bodies,
broad flat heads & flattened
femurs on the legs. Their gills
are like small plates with
bunches of filaments, attached
along the sides of the abdomen.
They grow about 15mm long.

**SLOW-SWIMMING NYMPHS**
like those of **Claret Dun**
*Leptophlebia vespertina* (**2**), are
typical of a large family of
mayflies, found in both still &
running water. They swim
slowly & with difficulty. They
are often dark brown, with
long, slender, forked or
feathery gills on each side of
the abdomen & very long tails.

**DARTING NYMPHS**
In another large mayfly family
the nymphs are agile swimmers
that can dart swiftly to safety.
They are slender, with feathery
tails & plate-like, almost transparent gills. They live in both
still & fast-flowing water. **Pond
Olive** nymphs *Cleoen dipterum*
(**3**) occur in ponds & lakes;
their adults are unusual in
having only one pair of wings.

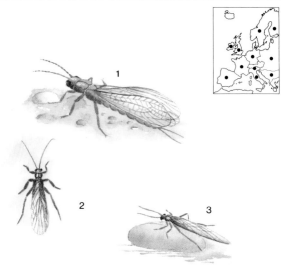

Soft-bodied, flattened insects with two long antennae. The two pairs of narrow, membranous wings have many veins. When at rest, wings are folded flat over the abdomen or moulded round the body. Larger species often have two long tail filaments.

Poor fliers, often resting on plants or tree trunks, or hiding under stones. Usually near unpolluted water. Trout feed on the females as they dip down to the water to lay their eggs. Most adults fly in spring and summer, living for less than a month.

The majority of species are found in hills and mountains, near fast-flowing streams, where the bottom is stony or rocky; a few live around slower-moving streams and rivers, fewer still on lake shores. Found throughout Europe and the British Isles.

**Large Stonefly** *Perla bipunctata* (**1**) is common near upland streams. **February Red** *Taeniopteryx nebulosa* (**2**) frequents weedy streams and adults fly from February to April. **Needle Flies** *Leuctra fusca* (**3**) wrap their wings around the body.

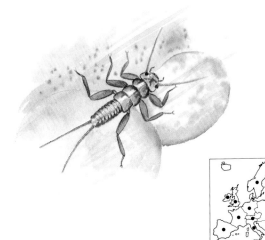

Nymphs are aquatic. They are like smaller, wingless adults, with two long antennae and two long, hair-like tail filaments. Many have tufts of thread-like gills on the thorax or near the tail filaments. Developing wing-buds can be seen on the thorax.

In the water the nymphs crawl under or around stones. Some feed on algae, others prey on worms and other insect larvae. They moult many times before climbing onto the bank to moult one last time, when the adult emerges. Empty cases may be common.

Found throughout Europe and the British Isles in unpolluted, well-oxygenated waters. Most live in fast-flowing streams in hills and mountains; a few live in slower-flowing streams, others on stony lake shores. Fishes, like Trout, feed on them.

**Large Stonefly** nymph (illustrated) is one of the largest; it is found in stony streams. In contrast to Stonefly nymphs, **Mayfly** nymphs (pp.71-73) have three hairy tail filaments. **Damselfly** nymphs (p.77) have three flattened, leaf-like 'tails'.

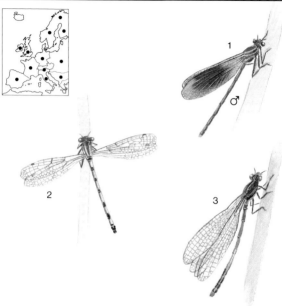

Smaller, delicate relatives of dragonflies. They have slender bodies and two pairs of membranous wings with complex veins. Wings are held over the body when at rest. Their heads and eyes are large, but the eyes do not touch.

Damselflies may be found resting on vegetation near the water where their nymphs develop. They fly in sunshine, with a weak and fluttering flight, and hunt other insects. Females lay eggs in water after mating and nymphs develop in water.

Found around rivers, streams, ponds, lakes and canals throughout Europe and the British Isles.

**Demoiselles**, like *Agrion virgo* (**1**), are broad-winged damselflies (three species in our area). Narrow-winged damselflies are much more common; they include **Common Blue Damselfly** *Enallagma cyathigerum* (**2**) & **Large Red Damselfly** *Pyrrhosoma nymphula* (**3**).

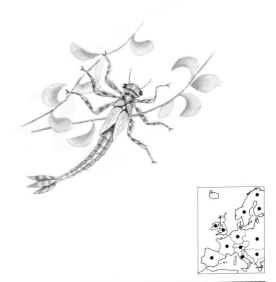

Long, slender, aquatic insects, with large head and eyes. The mouthparts form a mask like that of a dragonfly nymph. There are three pairs of strong legs beneath the thorax and wing-buds above. Three leaf-like tails are at the tip of the abdomen.

These nymphs (the damselfly young) develop slowly over the course of a year, moulting regularly, developing wing-buds as they grow. They finally climb up plant stems, out of the water in summer, to moult once more and release the damselflies.

The nymphs are slow-moving and they live among water plants in rivers, canals, lakes and ponds. They hunt like dragonfly nymphs, catching small creatures with the mask. The leaf-like tails function as gills.

In contrast, **Dragonfly** nymphs (p.80) have no tails, only sharp points at the end of the abdomen. **Stonefly** nymphs (p.75) have no mask and have two long tail filaments. **Mayfly** nymphs (pp.71-73) also have no mask and three long, jointed tail filaments.

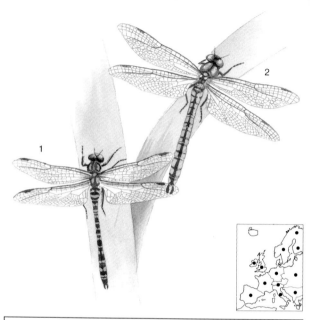

Large insects with long bodies. Two pairs of large membranous wings have complex veins. They are held horizontally to the sides when at rest. The head is freely movable with large eyes which meet at the top of the head; it has biting mouthparts.

Large predatory insects. They hunt other insects, like flies, on the wing. They fly fast and far in bright daylight (their wings making a rustling sound), often patrolling a definite route. Females lay eggs in water; and nymphs develop in water.

Found throughout Europe and the British Isles, most often near the water where their nymphs develop. Most species live around still and slow-moving water, rivers, canals, ponds. A few fly around faster-running streams. They do not bite or sting.

May have metallic colours, or black/yellow or black/blue bands. **Gold-ringed Dragonfly** *Cordulegaster boltonii* (**1**) flies around shallow streams but also ranges far from water. The fast-flying **Emperor Dragonfly** *Anax imperator* (**2**) frequents small ponds.

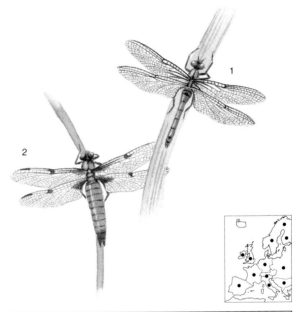

Large, stout-bodied insects. Two pairs of large membranous wings have complex veins; they are held horizontally out to the sides when at rest. The head is freely movable with large eyes which meet at the top of the head, and has biting mouthparts.

They often rest on plants beside water, then dart out to catch their prey, other insects. Their flight is fast and strong. They are most active in sunshine. Females lay their eggs in water after mating and nymphs develop in water.

Found throughout Europe and the British Isles, usually near the water where their nymphs develop. Most species are found around still and slow-moving water, rivers, canals, ponds. These dragonflies do not have metallically coloured bodies.

**Common Darter** *Sympetrum striolatum* (**1**) flies around still waters. **Four-spotted Libellula** *Libellula quadrimaculata* (**2**) is often seen around marshes. However, both species migrate far and wide, and may be seen far from water.

79

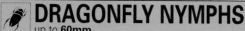

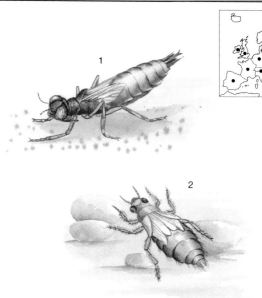

Stout-bodied, aquatic insects with a large angular head and large eyes. Mouthparts form a characteristic mask which folds beneath the head when at rest. Thorax has three pairs of strong legs and wing-buds. Abdomen ends in several sharp points.

These nymphs are the dragonfly young. They develop slowly over the course of one to five years, moulting regularly, developing wing-buds as they grow. They finally climb out of the water and moult once more to release the dragonflies.

Nymphs are slow-moving insects, found at the bottom of rivers, canals, lakes and ponds. They are ferocious hunters, catching small creatures with the mask; this is a large hinged lower jaw which can be swung out at lightning speed to catch the prey.

Nymphs of hawker dragonflies have a long abdomen, like that of **Emperor Dragonfly** (**1**). Nymphs of darter dragonflies have much shorter bodies, like that of **Common Darter** (**2**).

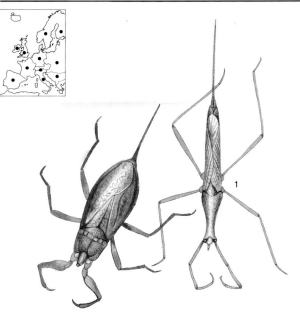

1

A dark, flattened, leaf-like bug with a long tubular 'tail' (actually a breathing tube, not a sting). Fore-limbs are grasping, like those of a scorpion, and can close up like penknives. Adult has wings but cannot fly. Feigns dead if handled.

A predator, hunting water insects, young fish, grasping them with the fore-limbs, sucking out the juices with the beak-like proboscis. Comes to the surface to absorb air through the breathing tube. Nymphs are like small adults, with wing-buds.

Found among the litter or half-buried in the mud, near the margins of ponds, lakes and canals. They look like dead leaves. Throughout Europe and the British Isles.

The related **Water Stick Insect** *Ranatra linearis* (**1**) is extremely long and thin. Though slow-moving, it catches tadpoles and insects with its fore-limbs. It lives among water weeds in ponds and lakes, often in deep water, throughout Europe and the British Isles.

These bugs look like boats with a pair of oars. They scull through the water on their backs, using their long flattened hind legs as oars. Adults are winged and fly from pond to pond. Eyes are red. They have a powerful beak and may bite with it.

Naturally buoyant, Water Boatmen may float, head down at the water surface with the legs and abdomen touching the surface. They are predators, hunting tadpoles, other insects, small fishes. Nymphs are like small adults with developing wing-buds.

Usually found in still weedy ponds, lakes and ditches, but also in slow-moving streams and rivers; they swim jerkily near the surface. Throughout the British Isles and Europe.

There are several species of Water Boatmen, all very similar. **Lesser Water Boatmen** (opposite) swim right way up, using their middle and hind legs; they live near the bottom.

Similar in shape to a Water Boatman, these bugs swim right way up, using the middle and hind legs as sculls. They do not bite. Adults are winged with striped wing covers. They can fly from pond to pond. Males trill loudly while courting a female.

Not naturally buoyant, they spend most of their time on the bottom, among stones or weeds, sucking up algae or plant debris with their beaks. They have to swim to the surface to get air. Nymphs similar to adults but smaller with developing wing-buds.

Found in weedy ponds, lakes and ditches, also in slow-moving rivers and streams. Throughout Europe and the British Isles.

There are several species of Lesser Water Boatmen, all very similar. The related **Water Boatmen** (opposite) swim on their backs with the hind pair of legs only. They swim just below the water surface.

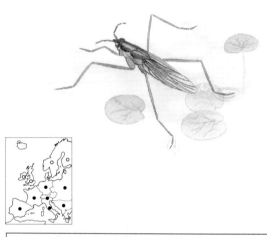

Bugs with long bodies and long middle and hind legs which rest on the water, making little dimples on the surface. Body is covered in thick velvety, waterproof hair which stops the insects becoming trapped in the water.

Pond Skaters are active predators, sensing insects trapped on the water, running over the surface and pouncing on them. They jump out of reach if threatened. Nymphs are like small adults with wing-buds.

Pond Skaters 'skate' on the surfaces of ponds, lakes, ditches, rivers and streams. Adults are usually winged and can fly from pond to pond; but some species have wings too small for them to fly. They are found throughout Europe and the British Isles.

There are several species of Pond Skaters, all quite similar. **Water Measurer** (opposite) is extremely thin and walks slowly over the water. **Water Crickets** (opposite) are much stouter.

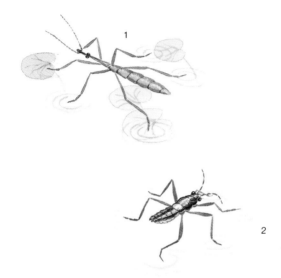

**Water Measurer** *Hydrometra stagnorum* (**1**) Up to 12mm long. Very long, extremely thin, wingless insect with long thin head. Eyes at the back of the head; antennae look like fourth pair of legs. It has long legs with which it walks slowly over the water, searching for insects on which it preys. It will jump if threatened. Body & legs are covered with thick waterproof hair which stops insect from getting wet. Nymphs are like small adults. Found on the water of still or slow-moving waters, ponds, ditches & streams, usually near the margin; also among the plants on the bank. Throughout Europe & the British Isles.

**Water Cricket** *Velia caprai* (**2**) Up to 7mm long. Water-walking bugs with stouter bodies than either Pond Skaters or Water Measurers. They are wingless. They are hunters, preying on insects caught on the water surface. Gregarious, often found in large numbers, usually near the banks of slow-flowing streams, also on mountain pools. Several species occur throughout Europe & the British Isles.

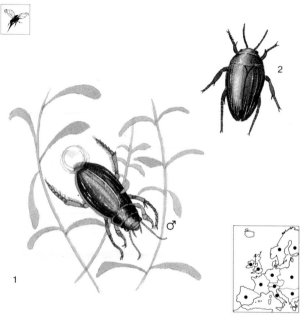

Streamlined, shiny beetles with smoothly rounded bodies, usually black or brown, often with yellow markings. The hind legs are fringed with long hairs and used for swimming. Antennae thread-like. Head is sunk partly into thorax.

These beetles are strong swimmers and fierce predators, hunting other insects, tadpoles and even small fish. They come up to the surface tail first to get air. They also fly well. Larva of Great Diving Beetle is described on p.90.

Found in all kinds of fresh water, ponds, lakes, ditches, canals, rivers and streams, from lowlands to mountains. Throughout Europe and the British Isles. They can bite.

A large family of aquatic beetles. **Great Diving Beetle** *Dytiscus marginalis* (**1**) is one of the largest and commonest. *Agabus bipustulatus* (**2**) is one of several similar smaller, but also common, species; many of them will fly to lights at night.

86

Streamlined beetles, silver-coated on the underside with a covering of air trapped by hairs. Most are black or dark brown; a few are yellow. Antennae short and end in clubs; palps are long and look like antennae. Legs not modified for swimming.

Omnivorous beetles, crawling among water weeds and browsing on them. They are poor swimmers. When they come to the surface for air, they come up head first, breaking the surface with one antenna. Larva of Great Silver Beetle is described on p.90.

Found in weedy ponds, ditches and slow-moving streams throughout Europe and the British Isles.

A large family of beetles, many of them aquatic. **Great Silver Beetle** *Hydrophilus piceus* (illustrated) is the largest but now rare due to overcollection. *H. caraboides* is very similar but only half the size and much more common.

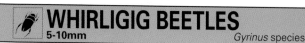

# WHIRLIGIG BEETLES
**5-10mm**

*Gyrinus* species

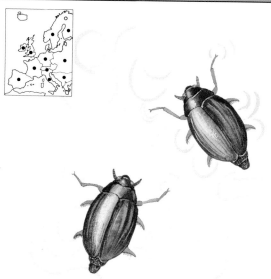

Small, black, oval, streamlined beetles with short antennae. Short, paddle-like middle and hind legs are used to scull them across the water. Their eyes are divided horizontally, the upper part for vision in air, lower part for vision in water.

These beetles swim erratically in intricate circles on the surface of the water. They swim faster if threatened, and will dive beneath the water. They catch mosquito larvae and other insects for food. The larva is described on p.91.

Gregarious. Mainly seen in late summer but present all year. They are found on still and slow-moving waters throughout Europe and Great Britain. They fly well and can soon move from one stretch of water to another.

There are several similar species of Whirligig Beetles in Europe; the one illustrated is **_Gyrinus natator_**.

**Screech Beetle** *Hygrobia hermanni* (**1**) About 10mm. Rounded, yellowbrown beetle which makes a screeching noise if handled (by rubbing its wing-cases against its abdomen). Found in weedy, muddy ponds in central & western Europe & the British Isles. The larva is described on p.91.

**Crawling Water Beetles** *Haliplus* species (**2**) Small, boat-shaped beetles (family Haliplidae), about 5mm long, pointed at both ends. Yellow or brown with black spots. Found in water with dense vegetation, mostly ponds or ditches, crawling slowly over plants or on the bottom. They feed mainly on green algae & any insects they can catch. Many species, found throughout Europe & the British Isles. Larvae are described on p.91.

***Elmis aenea*** (**3**) Up to 2.5mm long. A very small beetle, found under stones in the running water of streams.

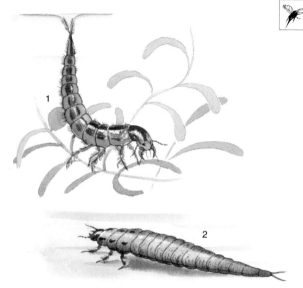

**Great Diving Beetle** larva
*Dytiscus marginalis* (**1**) Up to
5cm long. Spindle-shaped &
brown, with a round head &
well-developed legs. This larva
is an even more ferocious
predator than the adult, with
large jaws. It may bite! It hunts
tadpoles, small fishes & other
insects. Found among water
weeds in ponds & other still
waters throughout Europe &
the British Isles. It changes into
a pupa in spring, pupating in
the soil at the edge of the water;
adult stays in the pupal cell
until its body hardens.

**Great Silver Beetle** larva
*Hydrophilus piceus* (**2**) Up to
7.5cm long. Spindle-shaped &
brown but more fleshy than the
larva of the Great Diving Beetle.
It is rather flattened & straight,
with large jaws. A carnivore
(unlike the adult), hunting
snails, tadpoles, small fishes &
other insects. Found among
water weeds in ponds & lakes
in the southern British Isles &
throughout much of Europe but
rare (especially in the north).

# AQUATIC BEETLE LARVAE

Coleoptera

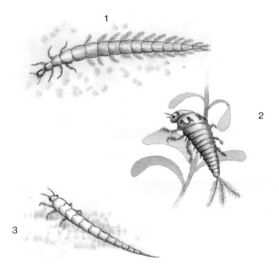

**Whirligig Beetle** larva *Gyrinus natator* (**1**) Long, slender larvae, up to 2cm long, with hair-like gills along each side of the abdomen. They live among water weeds around the edges of ponds, feeding on aquatic insects. They climb out of the water onto a plant stem in the latter half of summer, & there form the pupae, each inside a muddy cocoon plastered to the stem. Found throughout Europe & the British Isles.

**Screech Beetle** larva *Hygrobia hermanni* (**2**) This larva has a broad head & thorax, tapering

curved abdomen & three hairy tail filaments. It is found in the same places as the adult; & feeds on **Tubifex worms** (p.113). Pupa is formed in earth at the edge of the water.

**Crawling Water Beetle** larva *Haliplus* sp.(**3**). About 1cm long. Slender larvae, their bodies tapering to a point at the tail end; body segments have fleshy lobes with spiny tips. They live in similar places to adults & also feed on algae. Pupae are formed in the soil at the water's edge.

91

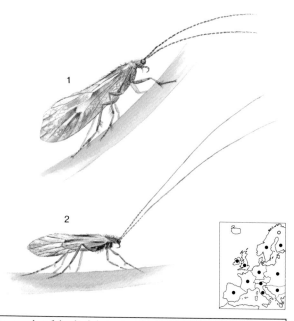

Elongated, soft-bodied, hairy insects, brownish in colour with no tail filaments. Two pairs of large, hairy, membranous wings are held in a roof-like position when at rest. Wings have few cross-veins. Antennae as long as wings or longer.

Mainly seen at dusk, often attracted to lights. These insects tend to fly poorly with an erratic flight. They hide by day in crevices or among vegetation and feed little. Females lay eggs in water or on overhanging plants. Their larvae live in water.

Many families of caddis flies occur throughout Europe and the British Isles. They are most often seen around water, all kinds from still lakes and ponds, to canals, rivers and fast-flowing streams. They may also fly further afield.

**Great Red Sedge** *Phryganea grandis* (**1**) is one of the largest; flies around still and slow waters in all but southern Europe. **Longhorn Sedges**, like *Athripsodes cinereus* (**2**), have very long antennae; they are common around lakes, ponds and slow-moving water.

Larvae are like caterpillars, with fleshy bodies, hard heads and biting jaws. They have three legs on the thorax and two strong hooks at the tip of the abdomen. Abdomen also bears thread-like gills. Antennae are so small as to appear absent.

Some are free-living, others make cases of stones, sand, shell pieces or plant fragments. Cases have a large front opening, through which head and legs protrude, and a smaller opening at the rear. The larva grips the case with its abdominal hooks.

Found in all kinds of fresh water, from fast-running streams to lakes and ponds. When the larva is full-grown, it seals the case (free-living ones make a cocoon), then forms a pupa. This goes to the surface or shore when ready, and the adult emerges.

There are many families of caddis flies in Europe and the British Isles. A variety of their larvae and their cases are illustrated on this and the next two pages. The free-living caddis larva of **Rhyacophila** is illustrated on this page.

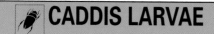
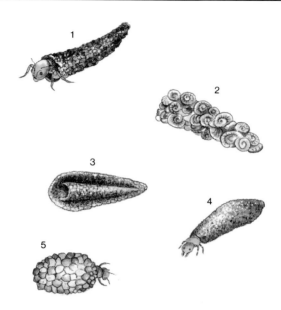

**CASE-MAKING CADDIS LARVAE**

Many caddis larvae make cases with small stones or sand-grains. They often live in fast-flowing streams & rivers, or on stony lake shores; their heavier cases help keep them from being swept away.

Some, like ***Sericostoma personatum*** (**1**) have curved cases formed of sand-grains; this species lives in fast-flowing, stony streams. Others, like many ***Limnephilus*** species (**2**) have straight cases of sand-grains or shells. ***Molanna angustata*** (**3**) builds a

distinctive sand-grain case, with a straight tube on a shield-shaped base; it lives in patches of sand or gravel in slow-moving rivers & lakes. ***Hydroptila*** species (**4**) build very small, drop-shaped cases of sand-grains. ***Agapetus*** species (**5**) have small cases made of stones, distinctive because the two openings to the case are on the underside.

Some caddis larvae make mixed cases, like ***Anabolia nervosa*** (no.1 on p.95); its case is made of sand-grains with small sticks attached to the sides.

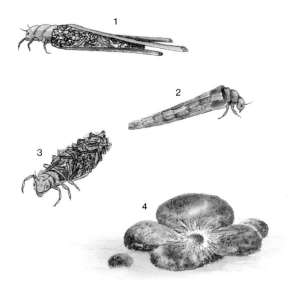

**CASE-MAKING CADDIS LARVAE**
Other caddis larvae make cases
out of plant fragments. Often
these larvae live in still waters,
where their lighter cases are
easier for them to drag around.
The plant fragments are often
arranged spirally into cylindrical
cases.

**Great Red Sedge** *Phryganea
grandis* (**2**) makes such a case
out of rectangular leaf pieces.
This larva lives in slow-moving
rivers & ponds. Other caddis
larvae arrange their fragments
tangentially, like ***Limnephilus
rhombicus*** (**3**); this species
lives in still, weedy waters.

**FREE-LIVING CADDIS LARVAE**
Not all caddis larvae make
cases; some are free-living.
Most of these live in stony, fast-
flowing streams, holding on to
the stones with large hooks at
the end of the abdomen.

Larvae of ***Rhyacophila*** species
(see p.93) live under the stones
in these streams. *Hydropsyche*
species larvae live in silken
burrows among the stones.
***Polycentropus*** species larvae
(**4**) spin silken funnels between
stones to catch their food.

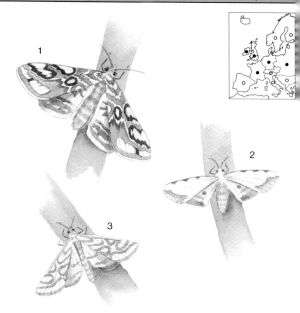

Small moths with narrow wings, named because the markings on the fore wings are said to resemble the makers marks on china. The palps on the head resemble a snout. Legs are long and spiky.

Most of the adult moths are terrestrial, flying by night or at dusk like most moths. But they are easily disturbed by day. In one species, the females may be wingless and live underwater. In all species the females lay their eggs in the water.

Several china-mark species occur in Europe and the British Isles. They are most common around still and slow-flowing water in mid and late summer, around river backwaters, ditches, ponds, where water lilies, duckweed and pondweeds are growing.

**Brown China-mark** *Nymphula nympheata* (**1**) and **Small China-mark** *Cataclysta lemnata* (**2**) are both locally common in central and western Europe, and in the British Isles. **Beautiful China-mark** *Parapoynx stagnata* (**3**) is locally common throughout the region.

# CHINA-MARK CATERPILLARS

Pyralidae

up to **25mm**

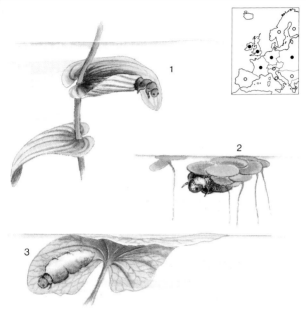

These caterpillars are like those of any moth, with three pairs of legs on the thorax and five pairs of prolegs on the abdomen. But they live underwater, living in cases that they make out of leaves. They are hairy, and the hairs hold air around them.

Some weave cases from Canadian pondweed or duckweed leaves. Others cut leaf pieces from water-lilies or pondweeds and sew them to the plants with silk, hiding in the cavity between. They poke their head out from the case to feed on the leaves.

Found in river backwaters, ponds and ditches, where water plants like water lilies, duckweed and pondweeds grow thickly.

**Brown China-mark** caterpillars (**1**) mainly make cases on pondweeds; those of **Beautiful China-mark** (**3**) on the undersides of water-lily leaves. They also occur on other water plants. **Small China-mark** caterpillars (**2**) make cases from duckweed leaves.

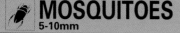

# MOSQUITOES
**5-10mm**

Culicidae

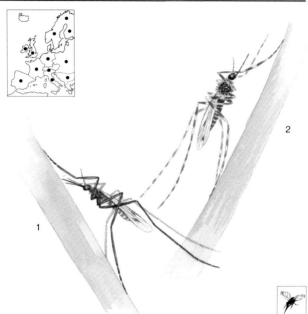

1

2

Slender, long-legged flies with a long, piercing proboscis. Females suck blood of people, mammals or birds. Males feed on nectar. Males have long feathery antennae, females have hair-like antennae. Hind legs are raised when they land.

There are two major groups of mosquitoes; anopheline and culicine. Anophelines rest with the head almost touching the surface. Culicines hold the body almost parallel to the surface. They all make a whining noise when they fly.

Mosquitoes are most common in damp places or near water, and most active from dusk to dawn. Anophelines and culicines are both common in southern Europe. Some anophelines carry malaria. Most northern and British mosquitoes are culicine.

Many malaria mosquitoes ***Anopheles* sp. (1)** have spotted wings; they occur throughout Europe but usually carry malaria only in the south. ***Culiseta annulata* (2)** is a large culicine mosquito with banded legs; it is often seen in houses and bites people.

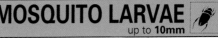

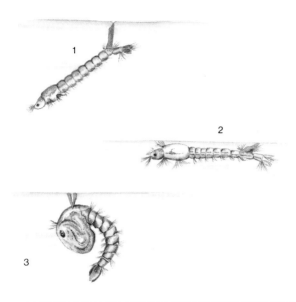

Wriggling, legless larvae. They have large heads, swollen thorax and long abdomen. At the tail end of the abdomen is a fan of bristles and there are other bristles over the body. Culicine larvae have a breathing tube at the tail end.

Female mosquitoes lay their eggs in water; the larvae and pupae develop there. **Culicine larvae (1)** suspend themselves at an angle from the surface of the water by the breathing tube. **Anopheline larvae (2)** lie horizontally beneath the surface.

Found in all kinds of still, stagnant or slow-moving water, including holes in trees, water-troughs, ponds, ditches and backwaters of rivers. Also in fens and marshes. Fishes feed on them. The larvae will dive, wriggling, if threatened.

**Pupae (3)** are comma-shaped with a large head and thorax. They also live suspended from the surface of the water, by a pair of breathing tubes, one each side of the thorax. They wriggle like the larvae. Adults emerge from the pupae directly into the air.

1

Fragile, slender flies; wings usually shorter than the abdomen. They have poorly developed mouthparts and no piercing proboscis. Humped thorax conceals the head from above. Males have feathery antennae, females hair-like antennae. ***Chironomus* sp.** illustrated.

Midges alight with the forelegs raised and rest with the wings held flat over the body. Many of them do not feed at all. They often appear in large swarms (of mostly males) over water in the evening. Females rest on vegetation nearby.

Found throughout Europe and the British Isles. Fish catch the adults as they emerge from the pupae, and also catch the egg-laying females.

**Phantom Midges** *Chaoborus* sp. (**1**) are related to mosquitoes but do not bite. They may be seen in late summer evenings around ditches, ponds and lakes throughout Europe. Their aquatic larvae are quite distinctive (see opposite page).

100

Many (but not all) midges have aquatic larvae like stiff worms, with small prolegs behind the head and on the last segment. They vary in colour depending on species. Most familiar are the bright red '**bloodworms**' of *Chironomus* species (**1**).

Female midges lay their eggs in water; many of their larvae build tubes of mud, and attach them to stones, shells, water plants, the sides of water butts. Others burrow into mud (like bloodworms) or live freely.

Found in lakes, ponds and marshes, in ditches, streams and the slower reaches of rivers, also in water butts. The larvae and particularly the **pupae** (**2**), which swim to the surface and hang there until the adults emerge, are important food for fishes.

**Phantom Midge** larvae (**3**) are transparent and difficult to see, lying motionless in the water of ponds and lakes, suddenly flicking away to catch water fleas and other small animals with their grasping antennae.

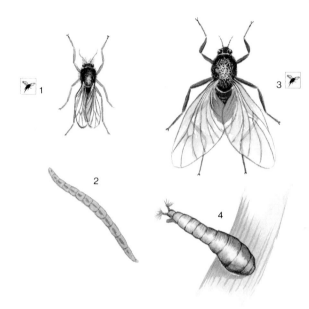

**BITING MIDGES** Ceratopogonidae
e.g. ***Culicoides* sp. (1)**
There are many species of these
tiny flies, all less than 5mm long,
with small heads & quite long
legs. Wings relatively large &
folded flat over the body when
at rest. Their **larvae (2)** are
slender & worm-like but stiffer
than worms; some are aquatic,
living in streams, marshes or
water-logged land; they swim
with a sinuous, snake-like
movement. Female flies bite on
summer evenings & can cause
much irritation. They may occur
in large numbers, especially in
northern Europe & Scotland.

**BLACKFLIES** Simulidae
e.g. ***Simulium equinum* (3)**
Very small, stout, black or grey
flies, less than 5mm long, with
short thick legs, short antennae
& humped backs. The females
bite horses, cattle & people.
Common near running water &
can be tormenting in hot weather.
Their **larvae (4)** are attached to
plants or stones in the fast-
flowing water of rivers & streams.
They form pupae inside little
open cocoons, attached in the
same way. Many species occur
throughout Europe, but they are
more of a nuisance in the north
& in mountains.

102

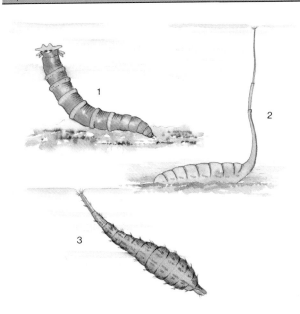

Several other groups of flies have species with aquatic larvae:

**Crane Fly** larvae (**1**) Although most crane flies (better known as daddy-long-legs) have larvae that live in the soil (when they are called leatherjackets), some, such as *Dicranota bimaculata* (illustrated), have larvae that live in streams & ponds, or around their margins. They can be recognised by the rosette of breathing tubes at the tail end. Like all fly larvae, they are legless.

**Rat-tailed maggot** (**2**) is the larva of the Drone Fly *Eristalis tenax*. It is virtually headless, usually grey & about 2cm long. It lives in rich black mud at the bottom of small ponds, getting air through the breathing tube which extends up to the water surface. Adult Drone Fly is a large hover fly, seen around flowers.

**Chameleon Fly** larva (**3**) hangs from the water surface by a tuft of bristles at the tail end of the body. It lives in ponds & ditches. The adult is a large soldier fly, *Stratiomys chameleon*, & may be seen sunbathing on flowers.

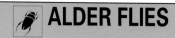

**Adults (1)** are about 1cm long. A dark, soft-bodied insect with two pairs of smoky brown, netveined wings, folded like a roof over the body when at rest. Antennae long & slender. They fly at dusk, resting by day on plants near water, but easily disturbed. They do not live long, emerging from pupae in spring & early summer. Females lay eggs on plants overhanging the water. Found near canals, slow-moving rivers, ponds & lakes, anywhere the bottom is muddy, throughout Europe & the British Isles.

**Larvae (2)** grow up to 25mm long. Each has a brown, elongated body, tapering from the head to a slender, fringed 'tail'. There are three pairs of legs on the thorax & seven pairs of pale, fringed gills on the abdomen. They live in tunnels in the silt or mud at the bottom of ponds, lakes, canals & slow-moving rivers. They are fierce predators, leaving their tunnels to hunt other aquatic insects or larvae. They live for one or two years, then crawl onto the bank in spring, to pupate in a chamber in the earth.

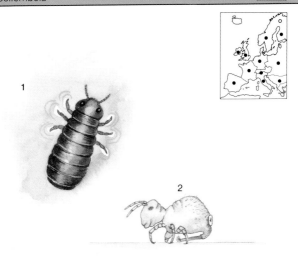

Tiny, soft-bodied, wingless insects. A tube protrudes from the first abdominal segment and a two-pronged 'tail' is bent under the end of the abdomen. Nymphs are like small adults and live with them.

Springtails have water repellant bodies. The tail is a springing organ, normally held by a catch but released if danger threatens; then the springtails jump away in all directions.

Springtails that live on the water surface are most common on duckweed; they live near the margins of ponds, ditches and streams, also in fens and marshes. Others live in damp places. They are found throughout Europe and the British Isles.

***Podura aquatica*** (**1**) and ***Sminthurides aquatica*** (**2**) are both common species. They may be present in huge numbers if conditions are right.

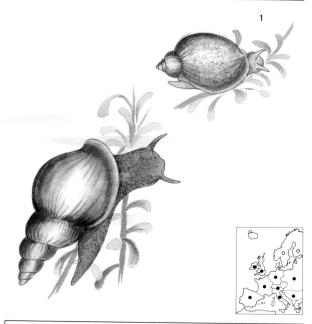

A very large snail, its shell thin and brown, with a large body whorl and a pointed spire. Aperture long and narrow, with no operculum. The dark grey body has a strong foot and the head has two blunt tentacles.

Even though they live in water, Pond Snails breathe air and must often visit the surface. Great Pond Snail not only grazes on vegetation but is also a scavenger on dead animals. Its eggs can be found in sausage-shaped, jelly-like masses under weeds.

Found among water weeds in ponds, canals and slow-moving rivers, usually where the water is hard. Throughout much of Europe and the British Isles, but not northern Britain.

Marsh and Dwarf Pond Snails are miniature Pond Snails (about 12mm tall); they live in marshes, ditches and wet meadows and are carriers for liver fluke in sheep. **Wandering Snail** *L. peregra* (**1**) grows about 2.5cm long; it is common in all kinds of freshwater.

106

# GREAT RAMSHORN SNAIL
*Planorbarius cornarius*  up to **2.5cm** across

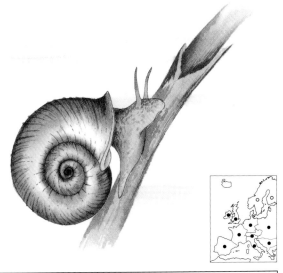

A distinctive snail, with its thick, solid, dark brown shell forming a flat, glossy coil of 5-6 whorls. Aperture has no operculum. Animal within is reddish-brown, with two long tapering tentacles.

Ramshorns breathe air and come to the surface like Pond Snails, but can also obtain oxygen from the water. They feed by grazing on water plants. Their eggs are laid in round jelly-like masses on water plants.

Found in large ponds and lakes, slow-moving rivers and canals, usually wher the water is hard. Locally common, most often in lowland areas, of the British Isles and Europe; less common in the far north and south.

One of 14 European Ramshorn species. Common Ramshorn grows up to 2cm across, and has a paler, matt brown shell; the animal within is blackish. It is common in shallow weedy ponds, lakes, rivers, canals and marshes, usually where the water is hard.

**River Snail** *Viviparus viviparus* (**1**) 3-3.5cm long. Robust, conical shell, green-brown with darker bands. Operculum present. Found among stones in slowmoving rivers & canals, usually in hard water. Central Europe, British Isles, north to Yorkshire. One of several similar species in Europe.

**Valve Snail** *Valvata piscinalis* (**2**) About 5mm across. Small, topshaped, rather flattened shell. When animal is 'out' it puts out a feathery gill. Head has a distinct snout. Found in gently flowing streams in Europe & British Isles.

***Bithynia tentaculata*** (**3**) 10-15mm long. Shell conical, glossy, light brown. Operculum present. Animal has long tentacles on head. Found in lowland rivers, canals, larger ponds & lakes, often on stones & in hard water. Much of Europe & British Isles except far north.

**Jenkin's Spire Shell** *Hydrobia jenkinsii* (**4**) About 5mm long. Small, dark shell with narrow pointed spire. Animal inside is pale grey. Operculum tiny. Found on stones & mud in estuaries & rivers. Most of British Isles & Europe, except far north.

**Bladder Snail** *Physa fontinalis* (**1**) About 10mm long. Shell pale, thin & shiny; body whorl inflated, with small, blunt spire. Operculum present. Finger-like projections of body extend onto shell when animal is 'out'. Found among dense water weeds in fast-flowing streams, ditches. Much of British Isles & Europe, except north.

**Nerite** *Theodoxus fluviatilis* (**2**) 5-10mm long. Shell egg-shaped & thick, with small spire, variable in colour (white to yellow or black), often marbled with purple. Aperture semi-circular, with shelf-like columella &

operculum present. Found in hard running water, on stones or plants. Much of Europe but absent from NW., also in England.

**LIMPETS**
Shells of these snails are thin & narrow, with low conical, curved spires. **River Limpet** *Ancyclus fluviatilis* (**3**) grows about 5mm long & lives in clear streams, rivers & lakes. Lake Limpet *Acroloxus lacustris* is smaller & flatter. Both live firmly attached to stones or weeds. Much of British Isles & Europe, except north.

Bivalve mollusc with thin, ovoid shell pointed at posterior end. Both valves have distinct growth lines and a thin brown 'skin'. Hinge lacks teeth. Two siphons barely protrude from hind end, foot protrudes from front end when animal is moving.

Found with front part of shell buried, siphon end protruding from muddy or sandy bottom. Obtains food and oxygen from water drawn in through siphon. Female produces millions of larvae which produce cysts in the skin of fishes.

Found in still or slow-moving waters of larger ponds, lakes, marshes amd rivers. Prefers hard water. Found throughout much of British Isles (except Scotland) and Europe except the north. Edible.

**Duck Mussel** *A. anatina* (**1**) is very similar but smaller (about 10cm long), darker and more swollen. It is often found with the Swan Mussel.

**Zebra Mussel** *Dreissena polymorpha* (**1**) 2.5-4cm long. Bivalve mollusc with two triangular valves; they have distinctive zigzag markings. Found in canals, slow-moving rivers, lakes & reservoirs, attached to posts, stones, docks. Much of Europe & British Isles, introduced from the Middle East.

**Painter's Mussel** *Unio pictorum* (**2**) 6-14cm. Bivalve with long narrow shell. Hinge toothed. Found in quiet, lowland ponds, reservoirs, canals & rivers (usually with hard water) across central Europe, also in England & Wales.

**Swollen River Mussel** *Unio tumidus* (**3**) 6-8cm. Similar to Painter's Mussel but shell swollen at apex. Found in quiet rivers, ponds & lakes across central Europe, England & Wales.

**Freshwater Pearl Mussel** *Margaritifera margaritifera* (**4**) 10-15cm long. Sometimes produces pearls. The two thick, kidney-shaped valves are blackish, with heavy growth lines, often eroded to show mother of pearl beneath. Found in cold clear streams with soft water & sandy bottom. Much of Europe, N. & W. areas of British Isles. Now relatively rare due to pollution.

# ORB-SHELL COCKLE

**1-2cm** across                    *Sphaerium corneum*

Small bivalve mollusc, with swollen, relatively thin-walled, yellowish, rather silky shell, like a small glossy stone. When active the animal extends two long, separate siphons.

Very common in mud or gravel, among water plants or climbing up their stems. Cockles move by extending the foot, gripping with it, then pulling the shell after. Water is drawn in through one of the siphons, bringing food and oxygen.

Found in all kinds of fresh water throughout Europe and the British Isles. Important food for ducks and other water birds; often the cockles grip onto their feet with their shells, and so are transported around.

One of several orb shell cockle species; some have harder shells. Several species of the related **Pea Shell Cockles**, for example *Pisidium cinereum* (**1**), are also common; they are smaller and their two siphons are joined. All these cockles have similar life styles.

112

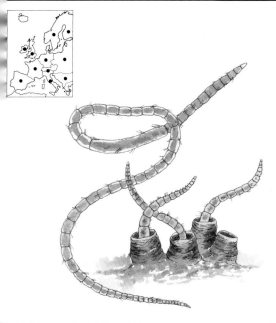

A long, cylindrical worm with many segments, like a bright red earthworm. Each segment has bristles on its ventral side. There is a swollen area (clitellum) about a third of the way along the body. Red colour comes from the colour of the blood.

Each worm lives in a tube, with its hind end protruding and waving in the water. At any vibration, the worms disappear into their tubes. They feed on organic matter in the mud, like earthworms. Eggs are laid in a cocoon produced by the clitellum.

A worm colony appears as a red smudge on the muddy bottom of slow-moving rivers, ponds, lakes, canals, sewage farms, even very polluted waters, throughout Europe and the British Isles. Food for ducks; used as bait by fishermen.

One of many aquatic segmented worms found in Europe and the British Isles. The white Pot Worms live among aquatic plants and mosses and resemble pieces of white root.

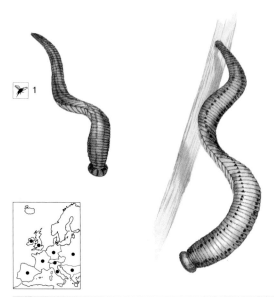

Tough-skinned, segmented worm with flattened body and two suckers. Large sucker at hind end, much smaller one around the mouth. Body very extensible. Back varies from pale yellowishgreen to blackish, with black flecks; underside paler.

Feeds on snails, worms, tadpoles, swallowing its prey whole. Swims by undulating the body. Also moves by holding on with its back sucker, extending its body and catching on to something with the front sucker, then letting go at the back.

Found throughout Europe and the British Isles, in the mud at the bottom of ponds, slow-moving streams and ditches, often under stones. Despite their name, Horse Leeches cannot attack horses or humans; their teeth are too blunt.

**Medicinal Leech** *Hirudo medicinalis* (**1**) has sharp teeth that cut through skin leaving a Y-shaped cut; it feeds on blood of mammals, including people. Nearly wiped out when used in medicine in the last century, but still occur in Europe and the British Isles.

# OTHER LEECHES

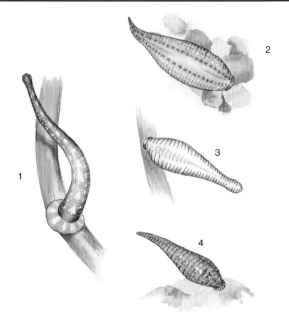

Most leeches are smaller than the Horse Leech & Medicinal Leech, usually reaching 1-3cm long, when extended.

## FISH LEECHES

There are several species of leeches which attack fishes in the British Isles & Europe. ***Piscicola geometra*** (**1**) has a very large sucker around the mouth & a greenish body with pale spots. It lives in fast-flowing streams & large lakes. It swims well, but often hangs on water plants, then fastens on to passing fishes to suck their blood.

## SNAIL LEECHES

Feed on snails & worms. ***Glossiphonia complanata*** (**2**) is a rather sluggish leech, found under stones in running water. ***Helobdella stagnalis*** (**3**) lives in the hard waters of slow-moving rivers & lakes. Both are found throughout the British Isles & Europe.

***Theromyzon tessulatum*** (**4**) lives in all kinds of freshwater except the fast-flowing upper reaches of rivers. It attacks ducks & other water birds, invading their mouths & throats, & can cause their deaths.

115

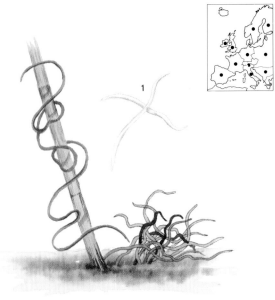

A thread-like worm resembling a large horse-hair. Yellow, brown or black in colour and often curled into tangled knots.

Adult worms do not feed. Females lay long white strings of eggs among water plants; larvae burrow into and become parasites in insects and develop into adults there. Adult worms emerge from these hosts when they return to water.

Found in still or stagnant ponds, even in horse troughs, also in ditches, slow-moving rivers. They may be absent one day, present in large numbers the next. They are found throughout Europe and the British Isles.

**Roundworms**, e.g. *Dorylamius* sp. (**1**), are a large group of related worms. Many are parasites but a few are free-living in fresh water. These are tiny (a few mm), and white with a thick cuticle; they move with distinctive, thrashing, S-shaped curves of the body.

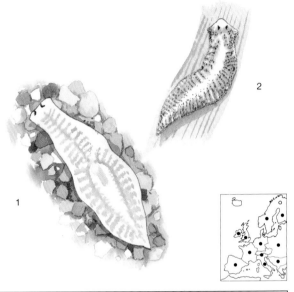

2

1

Soft, flat, unsegmented worms with eye-spots at the 'head' end, sometimes with tentacles. Mouth about half way along the body on the underside. The gut (visible through the skin) is divided into three sections. Colour white to brown or black.

Largely nocturnal, hiding by day under stones or plants. They move about with a characteristic gliding motion, but do not swim. They feed on eggs and small living animals or dead ones, detecting food sources from some distance away.

A number of species occur in Europe and the British Isles. They are found in all kinds of fresh water, from mountain streams and springs, to slow-moving rivers, canals, ditches and ponds. They can cause considerable harm to fish and frogs' eggs.

One of the largest is **_Dendrocoelum lacteum_** (**1**), found in mountain streams. **_Dugesia lugubris_** (**2**) is smaller (up to 20mm); it lives in lakes, ponds and streams. Planarians are related to Liver Fluke, a parasitic worm found in sheep.

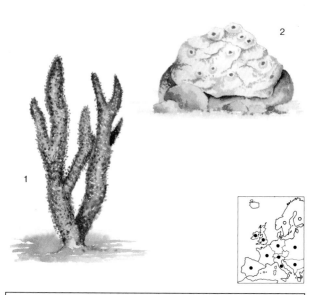

Sponges are simple animals, with many pores over their surface. They form tough, encrusting patches on various things in the water. Their real colour is grey-white or yellow-white but they may appear green and plant-like due to algae growing in them.

The sponges encrust stones, aquatic plants and roots, wooden posts. Water is drawn in through the smaller pores, sent out through the larger ones, bringing food and oxygen to the sponge. Many tiny water animals find shelter in the pores.

They live in ponds, lakes, ditches and other still waters, also in the deeper reaches of rivers. But are only found in clean, unpolluted waters. Found throughout Europe and the British Isles, except for the far north.

Two common species. Their names are misleading for **Pond Sponge** *Spongilla lacustris* (**1**) lives in the deeper reaches of rivers, often on canal locks; and **River Sponge** *Ephydatia fluviatilis* (**2**) forms patches on plants or roots in still waters of lakes and ponds.

# GREEN HYDRA

*Hydra viridissima*  about **5mm** (extended)

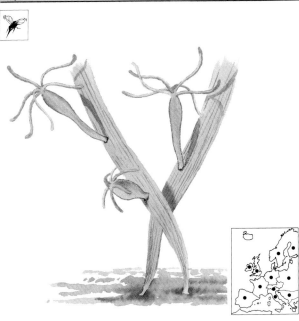

Small, cylindrical, sac-like animal, bright emerald green in colour.
When extended a mouth can be seen at the top, surrounded by a
ring of relatively short tentacles (shorter than the body). Tentacles
contain poisonous stinging cells.

Hydras catch small water animals with their tentacles, paralysing
them with the stinging cells and pushing them into the mouth. If
food is abundant, they reproduce by budding off new individuals.
They contract down to small blobs if disturbed.

Found attached by the base to water plants (and often difficult to
see because of their green colour), in weedy ponds, ditches and
streams. Throughout Europe and the British Isles. Can cause a rash
if they become entangled in fishing nets.

The colour of Green Hydra comes from green algae which live in
its cells. Brown Hydra is similar, with a similar lifestyle, but lacks
the green colour and is less common. Its tentacles may be four or
five times the length of the body.

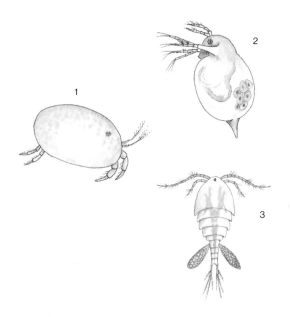

The animals on this & the following page are abundant in any sample of pond or river water. They can be seen swimming about if the sample is held up to the light. But a microscope is needed to see them clearly.

**OSTRACODS**, e.g. *Cypria* **sp. (1)**, are about 1-2mm long. They are tiny crustaceans resembling bean-shaped mussels, with a hinged, opaque carapace in two halves enclosing body. They swim by sweeping their antennae back & forth, or crawl on water plants. Many species occur in British Isles & Europe.

**WATER FLEAS**, e.g. *Daphnia* **sp.** (**2**), are 1-5mm long. Body visible through transparent carapace. Head has two pairs of large antennae & black eyes. Eggs often visible in a brood pouch. Swims by jerking the antennae. Throughout Europe & British Isles.

**COPEPODS**, e.g. *Cyclops* **sp.** (**3**), 0.5-2mm. Club-shaped body & two hairy appendages on the tail. Head bears one eye, a pair of small & a pair of large antennae. Females carry eggs in one or two brood pouches. Occur throughout Europe & British Isles.

# OTHER MICROSCOPIC ANIMALS

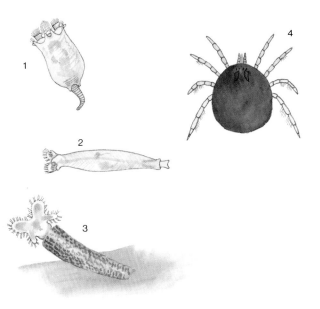

**ROTIFERS**

Microscopic animals with two circles of cilia on the head (that look like rotating wheels), a cylindrical, elastic body, & two 'toes' at the tail end. Some species are mobile, like ***Brachionus*** (**1**), swimming with the aid of the wheels; others squirm around on the bottom, like ***Rotaria*** (**2**); others, like ***Melicerta*** (**3**), live in tubes attached to plants. A few are colonial. Rotifers are abundant wherever there is fresh water. Several hundred species occur in the British Isles & Europe.

**WATER MITES**

Up to 8mm. Tiny animals related to spiders, many visible to the naked eye as coloured moving spots. They have an oval body & eight legs as adults (larvae have only six legs). Many are brightly coloured, like ***Hydrarachna*** (**4**) others are whitish. Adults are active creatures, & may be seen swimming purposefully about or crawling over water plants; larvae are often parasitic on other aquatic animals. Abundant in all kinds of fresh water. Several hundred species occur in the British Isles & Europe.

# Index and Checklist

Keep a record of your sightings by inserting a tick in the box.